the CREDIT REPAIR KIT

Fourth Edition

John Ventura

Dearborn™
Trade Publishing
A **Kaplan Professional** Company

This publication is designed to provide accurate and authoritative information in regard to the subject matter covered. It is sold with the understanding that the publisher is not engaged in rendering legal, accounting, or other professional service. If legal advice or other expert assistance is required, the services of a competent professional should be sought.

Vice President and Publisher: Cynthia A. Zigmund
Acquisitions Editor: Mary B. Good
Senior Project Editor: Trey Thoelcke
Interior Design: Lucy Jenkins
Cover Design: KTK Design Associates
Typesetting: the dotted i

Published by Dearborn Trade Publishing, a Kaplan Professional Company

Library of Congress Cataloging-in-Publication Data

Ventura, John.
     The credit repair kit / John Ventura.— 4th ed.
          p.   cm.
     Includes index.
     ISBN 0-7931-8060-0
       1. Credit ratings—United States.   2. Credit bureaus—United States.
     3. Consumer credit—United States.   4. Consumer protection—Law and
     legislation—United States.   I. Title.
     HG3751.7.V46 2004
     332.7'43—dc22

                                                                    2003019988

Dearborn Trade Publishing books are available at special quantity discounts to use for sales promotions, employee premiums, or educational purposes. Please contact our special sales department, to order or for more information, at trade@dearborn.com or 800-245-BOOK (2665), or write to Dearborn Financial Publishing, 30 South Wacker Drive, Suite 2500, Chicago, IL 60606-7481.

To my beautiful nieces Denise, Debbie, and Dana, of whom I am very proud.

Contents

Preface

A lot has changed since the first edition of *The Credit Repair Kit* was published in the early 1990s. For example, the three national credit reporting agencies have made their credit reports easier to read and now provide consumers with the option of ordering and viewing their credit reports online. Also, the federal Fair Credit Reporting Act (FCRA) has been amended twice. First in 1996 with the passage of the Consumer Credit Reporting Reform Act (CCRRA) and then in late 2003 by the Fair and Accurate Credit Transactions Act (FACTA). Some of the new amendments have been good for consumers; others have not. This book will tell you about many of them.

Other changes have occurred, too. For example:

- *The advent of identity theft.* If you are the victim of this fast-growing federal crime, your credit history may be destroyed. It could take you months, even years, to get your financial life back in order.
- *The use of credit scores.* More and more creditors and insurance companies are checking out your credit scores to make decisions about you rather than reviewing the actual information in your credit files.

- *Growing threats to your privacy.* Although the privacy of your personal and financial information has been under threat for years, new developments, including the advent of the Internet, amendments to the FCRA, and the passage of new federal laws, have made that privacy even more difficult to preserve.

Many things have stayed the same, however, since I wrote the first edition of *The Credit Repair Kit*. For example, consumers continue to have trouble understanding what their credit reports say about them and correcting negative misinformation in their reports. Inaccurate credit record information can be a serious problem, because it may cause you to be denied credit at reasonable terms, miss out on promotions and new jobs, be turned down for the insurance you need, and even lose the opportunity to rent the apartment you want.

Given all that has changed and all that has stayed the same, I believe that consumers need the information and advice in *The Credit Repair Kit* now more than ever. To respond to the changes, this new edition contains:

- Information on credit scores, including tips on how to raise yours
- A brand new chapter on identity theft, with step-by-step advice on how to avoid becoming a victim of that crime and what to do if you are
- Expanded information on consumer privacy and how to preserve it

The book also provides:

- A full explanation of your federal credit record rights
- Updated instructions on how to order your credit report from the three national credit reporting agencies—Experian (formerly TRW), Equifax, and TransUnion
- Sample credit reports from each of the three national credit bureaus and easy-to-understand explanations of how to read each report

- Time-saving sample letters that get results and create a paper trail that you may need later if you sue a credit bureau or creditor
- Information about government agencies and consumer group Web sites that can help you, together with addresses and phone numbers for these agencies and organizations
- Advice about how to rebuild your credit and use your new credit wisely
- Tips for how to minimize the financial repercussions of a divorce
- A discussion of the special credit-related issues women face and why it is important for all consumers, women and men, to have credit in their own names

As you can see, *The Credit Repair Kit* is not just for the financially distressed. It's for anyone who wants to be sure that they don't miss out on important opportunities in life because of credit record misinformation, identity theft, and other credit record problems. Following its advice will help you create a positive financial future for you and your family, full of opportunities and happiness.

Good luck!

Acknowledgments

Special thanks to all the people at Dearborn whose dedication helps make working with them such a pleasure.

1

How Credit Bureaus Can Affect Your Life

Margaret and Joe O. arrived in my office looking despondent. After saving for a down payment for several years and spending countless hours with their real estate agent, they had finally found their dream home. But they were turned down for a mortgage loan because of negative information in their credit reports. Now, they were meeting with me to get advice about what they should do next, because they were determined to buy a home for themselves. They arrived at the meeting with copies of their credit reports.

"We have worked hard to have good credit records, and we have always paid our bills on time. So, we don't understand why there is negative information in ours," Joe said. After reviewing their credit reports with them, I noticed that they contained information about a loan that Margaret and Joe had paid off and that they believed they had always paid on time. Yet, their reports showed that they had been late with their loan payments several times.

I talked with Margaret and Joe about their rights under the federal Fair Credit Reporting Act, including their right to have incorrect information removed from their credit reports. I also told them how to initiate an investigation into the information they believed was incorrect.

After a wait that almost cost the couple their dream home, their credit records were corrected. The lender who had supplied the incorrect information corrected its records, too.

Margaret and Joe were lucky because many consumers have difficulty getting misinformation in their credit records corrected. Even so, during the weeks that Margaret and Joe waited to learn the results of their investigations, they worried constantly about whether they would be able to get the loan they needed to buy their dream home.

Margaret and Joe's experience is just one example of how credit reporting agencies, or credit bureaus, can affect your life. It's also a good example of why you should review your credit record with each of the three national credit bureaus every six months, so that you can be sure that it is error-free and get any problems corrected right away. You should also review your credit record before you apply for credit you really need. If you don't, you may find yourself in the same situation as Joe and Margaret.

Congress passed the Fair Credit Reporting Act (FCRA) in 1970 to regulate the credit reporting industry and to give consumers certain legal rights in regard to their credit records and credit bureaus. Many provisions in the law also apply to the businesses and other organizations that provide information to credit bureaus and to the users of that information, as well as to specialty consumer reporting agencies that compile, maintain, and report information relating to consumers' medical records or payments, residential or tenant history, check writing history, employment history, or insurance claims. For the most part, these specialty reporting agencies are beyond the scope of this book. In 1996, the FCRA was amended with the passage of the Consumer Credit Reporting Reform Act (CCRRA). Some of the CCRRA's provisions expanded the rights of consumers and provided them with additional protections. However, other CCRRA provisions actually harmed consumers and benefited the credit reporting industry as well as providers and users of credit bureau information.

The FCRA was amended again in late 2003 with the passage of the Fair and Accurate Credit Transactions Act (FACTA). It too is a mixed bag for consumers. Among other provisions, for example, FACTA provides consumers with much needed rights to help protect them against identity theft and deal with the repercussions of that crime when they become victims—something that neither the FCRA nor the CCRRA does. FACTA also improves consumers' access to their credit record information and mandates changes to make those records more accurate. On the other hand, FACTA limits the ability of individual states to enact their own credit reporting and identity theft laws and to enforce many aspects of the law. It also limits the ability of consumers to enforce their credit reporting and identity theft rights.

As you read this book, three facts will become very apparent.

1. The information in your credit record—your credit history—can have a significant impact on your life, for good and bad.
2. Negative information in your credit record can limit your opportunities in life.
3. Many consumers discover inaccuracies in their credit records and then have difficulty getting them corrected.

For all of these reasons, it's important that you understand how credit bureaus work and what your legal rights are when you deal with them. This chapter will help you build that knowledge by providing you with basic information about credit bureaus, how they work, and about the various ways that they can affect your life.

What Are Credit Bureaus?

Credit reporting agencies or credit bureaus are part of a billion dollar industry. According to the Consumer Data Industry Association (CDIA), a trade association of credit bureaus, mortgage reporting companies, collection services companies, check services companies, and tenant screening and employment reporting firms, the industry consists of approximately 650 credit reporting agencies. Most of them are association members.

The majority of credit reporting agencies are owned by or affiliated with one of the three national companies that dominate the industry, and are linked to their computer systems. Those three national companies—Equifax, Experian (formerly TRW), and TransUnion—are often referred to as *the big three*. However, some smaller local and regional credit bureaus have no relationship with the big three. In addition, there are large, national information brokers that purchase consumer credit information from the big three and resell that information to other businesses.

Credit reporting agencies function as vast information clearinghouses on most American adult consumers. It is estimated that the three major ones maintain 190 million consumer credit files, enter 2 billion pieces of data into consumer credit files each month, and produce a whopping 1 billion credit reports each year. Credit card companies, banks and savings and loans, credit unions, finance companies, retailers, insurance companies, and the like purchase consumer credit record information from credit reporting agencies to help them decide whether to give a consumer new or additional credit, insurance, and so on. Employers and landlords may use this information, too.

What's in Your Credit Record?

Most of the information in your credit record (also referred to as a credit file or a credit report) provides a history of your use and management of credit. For example, it shows which companies have extended credit to you, whether you have paid your debts on time, and how much you currently owe each of your creditors. However, this history can change from day to day because credit bureaus are constantly collecting new information about you. Therefore, the credit record you review one week will probably not contain exactly the same information next week. A more complete discussion of the information in your credit record can be found in Chapter 2.

Where Do Credit Bureaus Get Their Information?

Credit reporting agencies obtain the information in your credit file from four basic sources.

1. *Subscribers.* Most credit bureau subscribers are creditors.
2. *Collection agencies.* Some of them are subscribers, too.
3. *Public records.* These include bankruptcy filings, tax liens, and court judgments.
4. *You.* When you fill out a credit application and provide information such as your name, current and former addresses, age, and Social Security number, that information may end up with a credit bureau.

Most credit record information is updated regularly—usually on a weekly or monthly basis.

How Can Your Credit Record Affect Your Life?

Your credit record can open or close doors for you and your family throughout your life, depending on the information in it. Among other things, it can affect your ability to qualify for new or additional credit and help determine the terms of that

WARNING

If an identity thief opens new credit accounts or obtains bank loans in your name and then defaults on them, this information will show up in your credit record and make it look as though you do not live up to your financial obligations. The negative information will lower your credit score, too. Chapter 10 discusses identity theft.

credit. For example, if a lot of negative information is in your credit record, you may still be able to qualify for a mortgage loan, but it will have a higher rate of interest than if your credit record was positive. Therefore, you will pay more for the home you buy over the lifetime of your mortgage.

The information in your credit record may also influence the kind of job you can qualify for, especially if you are applying for a job where you will be responsible for money or expensive equipment. It can also affect your ability to obtain adequate insurance and your opportunities to rent a nice home or apartment. Your credit record information may also prevent you from getting a government security clearance or a special license.

Credit bureaus also use your credit record information to generate your credit score—a single number that sums up how good a credit risk you are. Creditors are making increasing use of these scores in their decision making. Often, when you apply for new or additional credit, they never see your actual credit record, just your score. Credit scores are discussed in greater detail in Chapter 2.

Who Can See Your Credit Report Information?

The FCRA specifies who may review the information in your credit file and why. According to the FCRA, access to this information is limited to the following:

- *Creditors.* Creditors may review your credit record information when deciding whether to give you new credit, increase or decrease your current credit limit, or to change the terms of your credit. They can also review the information to determine whether to write off a debt that is past due or to turn over a delinquent account to a collection agency.
- *Insurers.* Insurance companies can access your credit record information when they are deciding whether they should sell you insurance of any type, how much insurance to sell you, and whether to increase the cost of an existing policy.

- *Employers.* Your current employer and potential new employers can review your credit record information when they are deciding whether to hire, fire, reassign, or promote you. However, they must get your permission first.
- *Potential investors, loan servicing companies, and current insurers.* These businesses can review your consumer credit record information to evaluate the risks associated with an existing obligation you have with them.
- *State or local child support enforcement agencies and state or local government offices that have been authorized by a child support enforcement agency.* These organizations can review the information in your credit record to help decide how much child support you must pay.

HOT TIP

A consumer reporting agency is prohibited from supplying a consumer's report that contains medical information to an authorized user for employment purposes or in connection with a credit or insurance transaction, unless the consumer consents to it being furnished, in connection with employment or credit. The consent must be written and the medical information furnished must be relevant or necessary to the employment or to the credit transaction. Also, the information supplied must relate only to the medical-related debts, accounts, or balances, and must be provided in a way that does not reverse the specific nature of the consumer's medical problem or treatment.

Your credit record can also be reviewed if:

- A business or individual has your written permission to do so.
- Someone gets a court order to look at it.
- The federal government suspects that you may pose a risk to homeland security.
- The IRS subpoenas the information.
- Someone has a "legitimate business need" to see your information in connection with a business transaction that you initiate. *Business transaction* includes the purchase of goods or services for your personal, family, or household use.

Insurers

Under the FCRA, insurers may review your credit record information before selling you insurance to make sure that you are not a high risk applicant. If you already have insurance, the insurance company can use the information to determine if it should increase your coverage, raise the cost of your insurance, or terminate your coverage.

Employers

If you apply for a job with a new employer or for a promotion with your current employer, the employer is entitled to review your credit record information as part of its decision-making process. However, the credit bureau will not provide the employer with information about your age or marital status, nor will it share your account numbers. Your current employer can also review your credit record information to help it decide whether it should take an adverse action against you—fire or demote you, for example. However, before an employer can look at your credit record information for any reason, it must get your written permission to do so. It must also provide the credit bureau with written certification that it has told you in writing that it may review your credit report as part of its decision-making process and that you have a right to a copy of the report.

If you do not get the job or promotion you apply for or if your current employer takes an adverse action against you due, in whole or in part, to information in your credit record, the employer must provide you with a copy of the credit report it reviewed as part of its decision-making process. In addition, it must give you written information about your FCRA rights, including the fact that you are entitled to have incorrect information in your report corrected or deleted. The employer must also tell you how to correct any problems in your credit record and provide you with the name, address, and telephone number of the credit bureau that generated your report as well as the credit bureau's toll-free number.

Government Agencies

Government agencies can take a look at your credit record to help them decide whether to give you credit, hire you, insure you, or grant you a special license or a security clearance. They can also use the information to help determine whether you qualify for government benefits like welfare and Supplemental

---

WARNING

Even if you tell an employer that your credit record is inaccurate, the employer can deny you a job or promotion, or take some other adverse action against you based on the information in your report. This is one reason why it is so important to review your credit record regularly and to clear up any problems right away.

Security Income (SSI), and the FBI can review your credit record in connection with an investigation. Also, because of September 11 and the federal government's concern about future terrorist attacks on the United States, government agencies can look at your credit file as part of an investigation into a possible homeland security risk. Otherwise, government agencies can only access the identifying information in your credit file, such as your name, address, and the name of your employer.

Legitimate Business Need

Before the 1996 amendments to the FCRA, the law included a provision that allowed anyone with a "legitimate business need" to gain access to the information in your credit file. Because the FCRA did not define that term, credit reporting agencies interpreted it quite broadly. As a result, they have turned consumer credit record information into a profitable commodity, using it to develop new products and services that they can sell to businesses. Many of these new products and services do not directly relate to the extension of consumer credit. Some of them are reviewed later in this chapter.

During the early 1990s, consumer advocates began to attack the buying and selling of consumer credit data, claiming that it was a violation of consumer privacy, and they argued that it was unfair for credit bureaus to make money off of consumers' personal and financial information and not pay them for the right to use the information. (The subject of credit bureaus and the buying and selling of consumer credit record information is discussed in detail in Chapter 9.) In response, the Federal Trade Commission (FTC) restricted the buying and selling of consumer credit record data and placed other limits on what credit bureaus could do with that information.

With the passage of the CCRRA, *legitimate business need* was somewhat more narrowly defined. Now, anyone with a legitimate business need for a consumer's credit record information can review it in connection with a business transaction that *the consumer* initiates, not in connection with just *any* business transaction involving a consumer as the law used to allow.

The CCRRA also allows creditors with a legitimate business need to access your credit record information to determine if you continue to meet their terms of credit. For example, the bank that issued you a MasterCard might review your credit record information periodically to determine whether it should modify your terms of credit—raise the interest rate on your card, or increase or decrease your credit limit, for example.

Another change to the FCRA as a result of the CCRRA amendments relates to prescreening. Prescreening occurs when a credit bureau compares the information in its consumer credit record database against a set of criteria that a creditor or insurance company provides to develop a list of consumers that the business can market its product or service to. However, the CCRRA says that a creditor or insurance company that purchases a prescreened list must make a firm offer of credit or insurance to each of the names on that list. It also requires credit bureaus that sell prescreened lists to offer consumers the opportunity to opt out of receiving prescreened offers by calling a toll-free number. That number is 888-567-8688. If you call this number, you will be opted out of prescreened offers for a period of two years. Chapter 9 provides more information about prescreening, including the prescreening-related requirements mandated by FACTA.

Another provision in the CCRRA that relates to legitimate business need applies specifically to bank holding companies and conglomerates and creates a huge loophole in the law. It says that these kinds of businesses can obtain consumer credit record information and then share it with their affiliated companies— companies that are a part of the same holding company or conglomerate. In turn, the affiliated companies can use and share that information with other companies, but when they do, they do not have to comply with most of the FCRA's consumer privacy provisions or with the law's requirements regarding information accuracy. In other words, rather than helping to protect consumers, this particular provision of the law actually helps bank holding companies and conglomerates circumvent most of the FCRA's consumer protections by creating, in essence, in-house credit bureaus that their affiliated companies can use and profit from. As a result, the consumer privacy provisions of the FCRA may not apply to countless companies. However, FACTA has attempted to close this loophole somewhat with a consumer opt out provision. This new provision is discussed in Chapter 9.

Credit Bureau Security

To prevent unauthorized businesses from gaining access to your credit record, businesses cannot become credit bureau subscribers without meeting certain criteria that prove they are legitimate businesses. Then, once a business becomes a subscriber, the credit bureau assigns it a special code and a security number that it must use to access consumer credit record data.

Despite credit bureau efforts to secure the information in their consumer databases, their security systems fail sometimes, and consumer credit record information has fallen into the wrong hands as a result. Although there is no 100 percent foolproof way to know whether someone who is not entitled to your credit record information has gained access to it, one way is to review the Inquiries section of your credit report. This indicates which businesses and other organizations have reviewed your information. If you don't recognize the name of a company or organiza-

---

HOT TIP

To help protect your credit record information, companies that purchase it for resale—information brokers—must provide credit bureaus with the name of the end user and explain how the end user will use the information. Furthermore, credit bureaus must have systems in place for establishing and certifying the identity of end users.

tion that appears in that section, contact the credit bureau that produced the report by initiating an investigation. You should also review your credit record regularly for signs that an identity thief has gained access to your credit record information and used it to charge on your accounts, open new accounts in your name, or obtain loans using your credit history. Chapter 2 provides more information about inquiries, Chapter 4 discusses investigations, and Chapter 10 discusses identity theft.

Investigative Reports

Although most consumers are not familiar with investigative reports, some credit reporting agencies produce them for companies, primarily insurance companies and employers. The reports provide subjective information about a consumer, including details about a consumer's lifestyle, personal habits, reputation, and character. The information in a consumer's investigation report is gathered through personal interviews with people who know him or her.

If a business orders an investigative report on you, it must notify you of that fact in writing within three days of asking a credit bureau to begin preparing the report and inform you of your FCRA rights related to investigative reports. Also, before the credit bureau can begin creating the report, the business must provide the credit bureau with a written explanation of why it wants the report. The business must also certify in writing that it will not use the report information for any other purpose and that it has provided you with all of the required notifications. In addition, the business must certify that if you make a request in writing, it will mail you a complete and accurate disclosure of the nature and the scope of its investigation within five days of receiving the request.

Before a credit bureau can include in an investigative report any public record information relating to an arrest, indictment, conviction, outstanding tax lien, outstanding judgment, and the like, it must verify the accuracy of the information. Also, credit bureaus are prohibited from including any negative per-

WARNING

As a result of FACTA, only post-employment uses of investigation reports are covered by the FCRA. The use of investigative reports during the hiring process are not covered by the law.

sonal information about you that they may obtain from your friends, neighbors, or associates without first trying to corroborate it through another source, unless the person who provided the negative information is the best possible source.

If you suffer an adverse consequence as a result of information in an investigative report, the business that requested the report must provide you with the name, address, and phone number of the credit bureau that prepared the report. You must also be provided with a written notification informing you of your right to obtain a free copy of the report and of your right to dispute any information in the report.

The Evolution of the Consumer Credit Industry

Credit records and credit reporting agencies were not always as important as they are today. Until the 1950s, businesses extended credit to people in their own neighborhoods or communities. As a result, most creditors knew something about the personal background, family, and bill-paying habits of the consumers they extended credit to and, therefore, did not have to use consumer credit reports. However, starting in the late 1950s, the number of national and regional consumer businesses began to grow, and, as a result, consumer-creditor transactions became increasingly impersonal. Consequently, a growing number of creditors looked to credit reporting agencies to provide them with the information they needed to make credit-related decisions about consumers. Also, the development and use of credit cards has made credit bureaus more important.

In 1970, Congress responded to changes in the credit reporting industry by passing the FCRA. This law helps to ensure that credit bureaus collect and use your financial and personal information in a way that does not violate your right to privacy and to guarantee you access to your own credit record information. Here is how the FCRA describes its purpose.

> . . . to require that consumer reporting agencies adopt reasonable procedures for meeting the needs of commerce for consumer credit, personnel, insurance, and other information in a manner which is fair and equitable to the consumer, with regard to confidentiality, accuracy, relevancy, and proper utilization of such information . . .

The Federal Trade Commission (FTC) enforces the FCRA and amendments to that law.

Figure 1.1 summarizes your rights under the FCRA. The complete text of the law, including all of its amendments, can be found at the FTC's Web site <www.ftc.gov>. You will also

---

HOT TIP

There are also specialized national consumer reporting agencies that compile and maintain information about consumers' medical records, payment history as tenants, check writing history, employment history, or insurance claims. The FCRA and its amendments also apply to these businesses.

FIGURE 1.1
Summary of Your Rights According to the FCRA, the CCRRA, and FACTA

The FCRA and its amendments grant you a number of important rights. The following list highlights some but not all of those rights.

- The right to know what your credit record says about you.

- The right to a free copy of your credit report every 12 month period from each credit bureau upon request.

- The right to know about the nature, substance, and sources of the information a credit bureau collects on you. However, a credit bureau does not have to share with you the sources of information it used to prepare an investigative report about you.

- The right to have your creditors tell you when they have reported negative information to a credit bureau.

- The right to know the name and address of the credit bureau responsible for preparing your credit report if you were denied credit, insurance, or employment or if the cost of your insurance or credit increases due in whole or in part to the information in your report.

- The right to a free copy of your credit report if a creditor or insurance company denies you credit or insurance or takes some other adverse action against you in whole or in part because of your credit record information. Be sure to request your free copy within 60 days of the date that you receive notification of the denial or adverse action. Otherwise, you will have to pay for your report.

- The right to a free copy of your credit report if you are unemployed and intend to apply for employment within the next 60 days, you are on welfare, you believe that you are the victim of credit fraud, or if you have been told by a collection agency that it has reported or may report negative information about you to a credit bureau.

FIGURE 1.1
Summary of Your Rights, continued

- The right to have an employer provide you with a free copy of your credit report before turning you down for a job or promotion or firing you due or partially due to information in your credit file.

- The right to have a credit bureau investigate information in your credit report that you believe is inaccurate or out-of-date. However, if the credit bureau decides that your request is "frivolous or irrelevant," it does not have to proceed with the investigation.

- The right to initiate an investigation directly with the provider of the information you are disputing.

- The right to have inaccurate information in your credit record corrected and outdated information deleted, when a credit bureau's investigation or an information provider's investigation finds information that you disputed to be in error.

- The right to have disputed information deleted from your credit report if you initiate an investigation and the credit bureau does not verify the accuracy of the information within 30 days of receiving your investigation request.

- The right to know the name, address, and phone number of anyone who has seen your credit record over the past two years for employment purposes and the right to know who has reviewed your credit record information for any other purpose over the past year.

- The right to have a credit bureau notify employers who reviewed your credit record over the past two years, or anyone else who looked at it over the past six months, of any corrections or deletions it makes in your credit file. However, you must explicitly request that the credit bureau do this, and you must provide the names of the companies and individuals you want notified. You may have to pay a fee, too.

(continued)

FIGURE 1.1
Summary of Your Rights, continued

- The right to have a brief, written explanatory statement added to your credit file when information that you dispute is not removed or corrected as a result of the investigation you requested. Then, whenever a creditor, employer, or insurer asks to review your file, they can read your written statement, too.

- The right to have most negative credit-related information deleted from your credit record after seven years.

- The right to have a bankruptcy deleted after ten years.

- The right to sue a credit bureau or an information provider in federal court, and under some circumstances in state court, if it willfully or negligently violates the law. If you win your lawsuit, you can collect attorney fees and court costs as well.

- The right to be notified when a business orders an investigative report on you, if you are employed by that business.

- The right to request that a business that has ordered an investigative report about you from a credit bureau provide you with more information about the nature and scope of its investigation, if you are employed by that business.

- The right to have a standard or extended alert added to each of your credit files using a one-call alert system.

- The right to have an active duty alert added to your credit file if you are active duty military or are a reservist who has been called to active duty and you are stationed away from your usual station of duty.

- The right to have information in your credit files that is the result of identify theft blocked.

- The right to obtain your credit score from credit bureaus for a "fair and reasonable fee."

find detailed discussions of your legal rights throughout this book.

The FCRA does *not* require that:

- A business or individual do business with you.
- An employer hire you or promote you.
- A federal agency intervene on your behalf.
- A credit bureau add to your file information on accounts that it does not ordinarily report.

Although most negative information in your credit file cannot be reported after seven years, there are exceptions.

- Bankruptcies can be reported for ten years. However, each of the big three credit bureaus reports successfully completed Chapter 13 bankruptcies for just seven years after the date of filing.
- Information about unpaid judgments that are the result of lawsuits filed against you can be reported for seven years from the date that they were recorded with the court or until the statute of limitation that applies to each lawsuit is up—whichever is longer.
- Unpaid tax liens can be reported for as long as they are not paid. However, the three national credit bureaus stop reporting them after seven years.
- Liens against your property that are not the result of a tax debt can be reported until they are paid or until the applicable statute of limitations is up—whichever is longer. Again however, the three national credit bureaus don't report these kinds of liens after seven years.
- Accounts that have been sent to collections can be reported for seven-and-a-half years after the date that the accounts first became delinquent, assuming they were added to your report after December 29, 1997. The same thing applies to foreclosures and repossessions added to your report after that date.
- There are no time limits on reporting information about you when you apply for a job with an annual salary of

$75,000 or more, for credit worth $150,000 or more, or for life insurance with a face value of at least $150,000.

How Technology Has Affected the Credit Reporting Industry

Starting in the 1980s, technological advances transformed the consumer credit reporting industry. For example, it evolved from a paper-based to a computer-based industry during this time. Also, technology made it easier for credit bureaus to collect information on consumers, produce credit reports, and use consumer credit record information to create new, profitable services and products for businesses. Some of these services and products help creditors evaluate, analyze, and monitor their consumer credit accounts, highlighting those that are at risk for delinquency or default. Others help businesses create highly targeted marketing databases. In fact, the money that the major credit bureaus make from selling credit reports to businesses and consumers now represents just a small fraction of the total revenue that they generate from their consumer credit record data. An overview of these other products and services follows.

Other Credit Bureau Products and Services Marketed to Creditors

The following list is not a comprehensive summary of all of the products and services that credit bureaus—mostly the three major companies—are now selling to creditors and, in some instances, to insurance companies. However, it helps illustrate the many ways that credit bureaus can generate income from credit record data besides by providing it to businesses and selling consumers copies of their credit records.

- *Fraud detection databases.* To help creditors detect fraudulent credit applications, credit reporting agencies have developed computerized systems that allow identifying information from credit applications, including online credit applications, to be compared with their fraud files.

When a match is found, the creditor is notified of the possibility for fraud.

- *Location finding.* Credit bureaus help creditors, landlords, collection agencies, and others track down missing consumers.
- *Collections.* Many credit reporting agencies offer collection services to their subscribers.
- *Credit scoring.* All three of the national credit bureaus produce consumer credit scores that are derived from consumers' credit record data. A credit score is a numerical representation of a consumer's creditworthiness. A growing number of creditors are making decisions about consumers based on their credit scores rather than by reviewing the information in their credit files. This means, among other things, that those creditors will never read the written statements that may be in your credit record. Chapter 2 provides more information about credit scores and Chapter 4 discusses written statements.
- *Account monitoring.* Credit bureaus help creditors minimize the number of accounts that are in default or delinquent by monitoring the payment histories and credit-use patterns of their account holders. They also let creditors know when new negative information has been added to the credit files of their account holders and when an account holder moves, changes jobs, and so on. Credit bureaus even monitor the performance of account holders with other lenders.
- *Periodic public record reporting.* Credit bureaus provide their subscribers with up-to-date public record information for their account holders, including data regarding federal and state tax liens, civil judgments, bankruptcies, and defaulted mortgages. Creditors use this information to help them pinpoint potential problem accounts, among other things.
- *Delinquency/bankruptcy predictors.* Credit bureaus develop and apply risk models and other risk evaluation methods to the consumer information in their databases

in order to help creditors identify consumers who are most at risk for falling behind on their payments, defaulting on their accounts, or filing for bankruptcy.

- *Prescreening.* Credit bureaus create highly targeted marketing lists for creditors and for insurance companies by matching up the information in their consumer credit files, including information regarding consumers' spending and payment patterns, with specific criteria provided by the businesses. In turn, the creditors and insurance companies market specific products and services, promotions, and so on to the names on those lists.

- *Database enhancement.* Credit bureaus help businesses improve their marketing databases by selling them specific information about the consumers in those databases.

Criticism of Credit Reporting Agencies

During the late 1980s and early 1990s, consumer watchdog groups, policy makers, state attorneys general, the media, and consumers themselves were highly critical of the credit reporting industry and pushed for reform. They criticized the industry because:

- There was a high rate of error and inaccuracy in consumer credit files, although to be fair, some of these problems were because the information that creditors provided to the credit bureaus was not always accurate or up-to-date.

- Consumers were having problems getting the misinformation in their credit records corrected.

- Some credit bureaus were mistakenly comingling information from one consumer's credit file with information from someone else's with a similar name. In other words, the negative information in one person's credit file was contaminating someone else's file.

- Credit bureaus were collecting, storing, and reselling massive amounts of sensitive, highly personal information about consumers, usually without their knowledge.

HOT TIP

It is illegal for information providers to knowingly supply erroneous information to credit reporting agencies.

These problems were addressed in several ways. First, attorneys general in several states and the Federal Trade Commission (FTC) became more aggressive with credit bureaus and creditors who violated the law. In some instances, they filed lawsuits against them. Also, credit reporting agencies initiated their own changes in regard to how they dealt with consumers and the way that they did business in general. In addition, after numerous false starts, Congress strengthened the FCRA by passing the CCRRA, which among other things requires credit bureaus to give consumers the option to opt out of prescreening. FACTA added additional rights for consumers when it comes to prescreening. Yet, despite all of these changes, many consumers continue to have problems with credit bureaus; the information in their credit files continues to be a lucrative source of income for the three national credit bureaus; and issues related to consumer privacy and identity theft continue to be of concern to consumers, policy makers, and consumer watch dog groups.

Penalties for Violating Your Federal Credit Record Rights

If a credit bureau or supplier/user of credit bureau information violates your legal rights under the FCRA, the CCRRA, or FACTA, you may be entitled to do the following:

- Sue in civil court for *willful noncompliance*, which means that you believe the credit bureau or information provider/user willfully and knowingly violated the law.

However, proving willful noncompliance can be hard to do. You can sue for the greater of actual damages or statutory damages of not less than $100 and not more than $1,000, plus attorney fees. The court may also award you punitive damages if you win your lawsuit, assuming you are able to prove that you were harmed in some way by the credit bureau and/or information provider/user. For example, you incurred expenses you would not have incurred otherwise, you lost income because you had to take unpaid time off from work to deal with your credit record problem, or you experienced pain and suffering as a result of the credit bureau's action.

- Sue for *negligent noncompliance*. When you make negligent noncompliance the basis of your lawsuit, you are alleging that a credit bureau or supplier/user of credit bureau data made a mistake that harmed you in some way, but that the mistake was not intentional. You can sue for actual damages plus attorney fees.

- Sue for a minimum of $1,000, attorney fees, and punitive damages if someone obtains a copy of your credit report under false pretenses. According to the FCRA, anyone who does will be subject to fines or imprisonment of up to two years. Similar penalties apply to an employee or an officer of a credit bureau who provides information from your credit file to an unauthorized user.

If you are having problems getting a problem in your credit record corrected or if you are having other problems with a credit bureau, an information provider, or a user of your credit record information, schedule an appointment with a consumer law attorney sooner rather than later. The attorney should be someone who has specific experience representing consumers in credit record-related matters. The attorney can help you resolve your problem a lot more quickly than you could and spare you considerable frustration and worry at the same time. Also, if the attorney feels that you have a good basis for a lawsuit, he

> ## HOT TIP
>
> The National Association of Consumer Advocates (NACA) is a good resource for locating a consumer law attorney in your area who has plenty of experience handling credit record legal problems. Contact NACA at 202-452-1989 for a referral to a consumer law attorney.

or she will tell you what to do and what not to do to build your case. This information can be invaluable.

If the consumer law attorney believes that you have a good case, they will probably take it on contingency, which means that you will not have to pay the lawyer a fee unless you win your lawsuit. The attorney will take the fee out of whatever money the court awards you. However, win or lose, you will probably have to reimburse the attorney for out-of-pocket expenses.

Chapter 4 in this book provides more information about hiring a consumer law attorney and suing a credit bureau or a supplier or user of information in your credit file.

2

Credit Records and Credit Scores: How to Find Out about Yours

Constance M. was referred to me by a mutual friend. Constance was in her late twenties and a manager in a small software design firm. She was meeting with me, not because of financial problems, but because she had read an article advising all consumers to review their credit records every six months for errors and for signs that they were the victims of identity theft. Constance had gone ahead and ordered her credit record. Now, she wanted my help understanding how to read it because she had never seen a copy of her credit report before.

Constance was relieved after we completed the review of her credit report because it showed that she had managed her credit well, that it contained no misinformation, and that she was not the victim of identity theft. However, I told Constance that there were three national credit bureaus, that all of them were probably maintaining a credit file on her, and that it was very likely that the information in each file differed somewhat. I also explained that just because the report from one credit bureau was problem free, there was no guarantee that the reports of the other two credit bureaus would not have problems. Therefore, I advised her to order a copy of her credit record from those other credit bureaus. I also told Constance about the growing importance of credit scores and how to order hers.

This chapter gives you the information you need to order a copy of your credit record from each of the three national credit bureaus and highlights the information you will find in it. It also explains what a credit score is, tells you how to find out your score, and provides you with advice for improving it.

If you have a good credit history, checking these records every six months is a wise preventive measure. That way, you will know when you need to address problems, and you can find out if someone has stolen your identity and gotten credit in your name. You should also order copies of your credit reports before you apply for credit or insurance that you really need, for a new job or promotion, or for a place to rent, because your credit record may be reviewed as part of the application process. That way, you will know ahead of time if there are problems that might cause your application to be denied, and you can take steps to correct the problems.

Order Your Report from All Three National Credit Bureaus

If you want to have a comprehensive picture of how you are being portrayed as a consumer, you should obtain a copy of your credit report from each of the three national credit reporting agencies—Equifax, Experian, and TransUnion—not from just one. This is important advice because credit bureaus obtain much of the information they have in their consumer credit files from the creditors that subscribe to their services. Because not every information provider works with the same credit bureaus, the information in your credit file may vary somewhat from one credit bureau to another. For example, Company A may report to Experian and Equifax, but Company B may just report to TransUnion, and Company C may report only to Experian. However, most large creditors now report data to each of the three national credit bureaus.

For these reasons, therefore, it is becoming more and more likely that your Equifax, Experian, and TransUnion credit reports will list the same credit accounts and public record information. On the other hand, it also means that if a subscriber provides inaccurate information about a consumer to one of the national credit bureaus, that same information may also turn up in the files of the other two. Bottom line: if you want a complete picture of how you are being portrayed as a credit user, regularly review all your credit reports—from Equifax, Experian, and TransUnion.

How to Request a Copy of Your Credit Report from Each of the Big Three

You can order a copy of your credit report from the three national credit bureaus in one of three ways. You can:

1. Go to their Web sites and order online.
2. Call their toll-free numbers.
3. Send them a request letter.

WARNING

These options and the descriptions that follow later in the chapter *do not* apply when you are ordering the free annual reports you are now entitled to under FACTA. In fact, if you use them to order your free reports rather than ordering through the centralized resource mandated by FACTA, the credit bureaus have the right to refuse to process your requests. The free annual reports are discussed later in this chapter.

The three national credit bureaus prefer that you order your credit reports online. Here's why.

- *It takes less time.* Ordering online is faster than ordering by telephone or using the mail. In fact, if you order online, you can obtain your report instantly.
- *It's more secure.* When you use the mail to request your credit record, you are at a greater risk of becoming a victim of identity theft than if you order over the phone or online. This is because many people will have access to the identifying information in your credit record request letter and in your credit report. However, if you call a credit bureau's toll-free line to order your report, your identifying information will be better protected because you will be dealing with an automated system. Therefore, your information will have fewer opportunities to fall into the wrong hands. If you order online, your information is protected, because the Web sites of the three national credit bureaus use security technology.
- *You will know exactly how much you must pay for your report.* If you order your report by phone or online, both ordering systems will automatically provide you with the correct fee for your report. This service is very helpful, both because the cost of a credit report changes periodically and because consumers in some states are entitled to one or more free or lower-cost credit reports

---

H O T   T I P

If you request your credit file but not your credit score as well, the credit reporting agency you ordered from must advise you that you can order your credit score too.

each year. If you request your credit report by mail and you send the wrong amount of money with your letter, there will be a delay in processing your request while the credit bureau notifies you of the correct fee and you resend your request.

The Cost of Your Credit Report

With the passage of FACTA, you are now entitled to receive one free copy of your credit report for each credit reporting agency during any 12-month period. (You are also entitled to receive a free annual report from each of the national specialized consumer reporting agencies.) Credit reporting agencies must provide you with your free report within 15 days of receiving your request. At the time this book was written, the exact method for ordering the report had not been determined, although the law states that you must order it through a "centralized source." You can order through this source through the mail, phone, or Internet. Also, the date on which this new provision will go into effect had not been determined. In fact, given that way FACTA is worded, it is possible that free annual reports for all consumers who request them may not be a reality until December 4, 2004, although the process may be in place sooner. (Free specialized reports may not be available until March 4, 2005.) However, once a centralized source has been established and a request has been set up, that information will be available for free at the author's Web site <www.johnventura.com>.

You are also entitled to a free credit report if any of the following apply to you:

- You were denied credit, employment, insurance, or housing.
- You are the victim of fraud.
- You are unemployed and intend to apply for work within 60 days.
- You are on welfare.
- You believe that you are the victim of credit fraud.

- A collection agency tells you that it has reported, or may report, negative information about you to a particular credit bureau.

If you have ordered your free annual reports under FACTA from each of the national credit reporting agencies and you want to obtain additional reports during the same year, unless one of the preceding bullet points apply to you, you will have to pay $9 per report, although periodically the cost is increased. However, depending on your state of residence, you may be able to obtain additional free or reduced price reports during the same year even if the bullet points do not apply to you.

HOT TIP

Residents of ten states (Colorado, Connecticut, Georgia, Maine, Maryland, Massachusetts, Minnesota, Montana, New Jersey, and Vermont) may be able to obtain additional copies of their credit reports for free or for a reduced price, under their state's credit reporting law, in the same year that they obtain their free FACTA report. At the time this book was written, the FTC, which enforces the FCRA and all its amendments, was not clear about whether FACTA pre-empted those other states laws. Once clarification is available, you can find it at the author's Web site, JohnVentura.com. Your state attorney general's office of consumer protection should also be able to provide the information once it is available.

WARNING

Unless you request your free report within 60 days of an adverse action, you will have to pay for the report, assuming your state does not entitle you to one or more free reports each year and you have not already used up your quota of free reports.

Ordering by Phone

Each of the three national credit bureaus has a national toll-free line for ordering a copy of your credit report when you are ordering additional copies of your credit report in a given year for any reason. You will have to pay for it with a MasterCard, Visa, American Express, or Discover card. When you call a toll-free number, a series of messages will guide you through the ordering process and tell you how much your report will cost. The numbers to call to order your report are:

Equifax	800-685-1111 or 888-397-3742
Experian	888-397-3742
TransUnion	800-888-4213

Ordering Online

For the fastest service when ordering additional copies of your credit report in a given year for any reason, order your credit reports online by going to the Web sites of the big three. Once you pay with a MasterCard, Visa, American Express, or Discover card, you can view your credit report instantly and print it off.

The Web sites of the three national credit bureaus are:

Equifax	<www.equifax.com>
Experian	<www.experian.com/yourcredit>
TransUnion	<www.transunion.com>

Ordering by Mail

If you decide to order your credit report through the mail despite the potential drawbacks, you must include very specific information in your letter. If you omit any of it, fulfillment of your request will be delayed. Provide the following information:

- Your full name, including your middle name. Be sure to include Jr., Sr., III, and so forth if applicable
- Your spouse's name, if you're married
- Your date of birth
- Your Social Security number
- Your current address and former address, if you haven't lived at your current address for at least five years
- The name of your current employer
- Your daytime and evening phone numbers with area codes

To prove your identity and current address and to help the credit bureau locate you in its database, enclose a copy of one

WARNING

If you hand write your letter, make sure that all of your words are legible. Otherwise, there will be a delay in processing your request if the credit reporting agency has to contact you to clarify what you wrote.

of the following: your billing statement from a major national bank card or from your American Express card, a copy of a recent utility bill, a copy of your driver's license, or a copy of some other bill or document that shows your name and current address. Last but not least, be sure to sign your letter.

If you request a copy of your credit report because you have been denied credit, insurance, or employment, or experienced some other adverse action, you are entitled to receive a free copy of your credit report from the company that reported the information. However, you must request your free copy within 60 days of the adverse action. If you wait longer than 60 days to order your report, include a check or money order in the appropriate amount with your letter. After the credit bureau receives your request, it should respond within three business days. Figure 2.1 provides a sample letter that you can use as a model for your own letter.

Send your request letter to

Equifax
Disclosure Department
PO Box 740241
Atlanta, GA 30374-0241

HOT TIP

When you write to request a free report because you were denied credit, employment, etc., or experienced some other adverse action, attach a copy of the notice you received informing you of the adverse action. However, if you don't have the notice, make your request anyway.

Experian
National Consumer Assistance Center
PO Box 2002
Allen, TX 75013-2104

FIGURE 2.1
Sample Credit Report Request Letter

(Date)
(Address of Credit Bureau)

Dear Sir or Madam:

I am writing to request a copy of my credit report.
My complete name is:
My Social Security number is:
My date of birth is:
My spouse's complete name (if applicable) is:
My spouse's Social Security number is:
My current address (do not use a PO Box number):
My previous address(es) over the past five years are:
My employer is:
My daytime phone number is: (area code and telephone number)
My evening phone number is: (area code and telephone number)
To pay for the cost of my report, I have enclosed a check (or money order) for
$_____.
Please send the report to me at the following address:

Thank you for your cooperation. If you have any questions, you may contact me at:
(area code and telephone number).

Sincerely,

(Signature)

TransUnion
Consumer Disclosure Center
PO Box 1000
Chester, PA 19022-1000

Ordering a Copy of Your Credit Record from a Local or Regional Credit Bureau

Although their numbers are declining, there may be a local or regional credit bureau in your area that is not affiliated with any of the national credit reporting agencies. To find out if any of them have a credit file on you, look in your local Yellow Pages under *credit reporting agencies* or *credit bureaus*. If you see any listings, jot down an address and telephone number for each. Then call the credit bureaus on your list to find out if they are affiliated with one of the national credit bureaus. When you find one that is not, ask how you can learn whether it is maintaining a file on you and how to order a free copy of that file.

What's in a Credit Report?

All credit reports contain the same basic types of information: identifying data, credit history, inquiries, and public record data. However, each credit reporting agency uses a different format for presenting this information. Therefore, some reports are easier to understand than others. For example, Experian's credit report is particularly easy to read because it is free of confusing codes and symbols and uses a narrative format to present consumer account information. The version you receive if you order your report by phone or mail also features an initial summary page that indicates the number of creditor accounts and public record items in your credit record that contain negative information. That page also clearly highlights the number to call and the Web site to visit if you want to dispute information in your credit report, need assistance from Experian, or want to order a copy of your credit score. (Credit scores are discussed later in this chapter.) The report comes with a form to complete if you find incorrect information and want Experian to correct or delete it.

The TransUnion credit report is slightly less consumer friendly but, like Experian's report, it highlights any negative information. It also comes with a form to complete and return to TransUnion if you disagree with information in your report and want it corrected or deleted. Also, at the end of the report, TransUnion provides a Web site address for initiating an investigation online and a toll-free number to call for assistance.

Of the three, the Equifax credit report uses the most codes and symbols to present information. Therefore, it is the least consumer friendly.

Chapter 3 explains how to understand the information in your Equifax, Experian, and TransUnion credit reports. But, if you are still confused after you read that chapter, contact the credit bureau that produced your credit report. The FCRA requires that all credit bureaus have personnel available to answer questions and help consumers interpret the information in their credit reports. Call the toll-free numbers earlier in this chapter provided for each of the big three, unless your credit report provides an alternative number to call.

Identifying Data

The identifying information in your credit report usually includes the following, although it varies somewhat from credit bureau to credit bureau:

- Name, including any nicknames you may have used to apply for credit (such as Bill instead of William), and whether you are a Jr., a Sr., a III, a IV, and so on
- Current and previous addresses
- Birth date
- Spouse's name
- Current and previous employers
- Social Security number
- Your phone number

This information generally comes from credit and loan applications that you have filled out.

Credit History

The heart of any credit report is the section containing payment history information for each of the credit accounts being reported. Despite their slightly different formats, you should expect to find the following types of account information in your Equifax, Experian, and TransUnion reports:

- Name of the creditor and account/loan number
- Nature of the account/loan—whether it is joint or individual
- Type of account/loan—whether it is a revolving or installment account, a student loan, or a mortgage, for example
- Date account was opened or loan was established
- Credit limit on the account or the loan amount
- Current balance on the account/loan. Note: The dollar amount shown in this section of your report will reflect the account balance at the time the information was reported to the credit bureau. It will not reflect any payments or charges you may have made since that date.
- The most you have owed on the account/loan
- How much you are required to pay each month on the account/loan for the period being reported
- Your account payment history. This information will probably include the payment status of the account/loan as of the date it was reported to the credit bureau, the number of times you were late paying on the account/loan during a certain period of time (the period of time varies from account to account), whether the account/loan was closed at your request or by the creditor, and whether it was referred to collections.
- Date information on the account/loan was last reported to the credit bureau
- Number of months for which information has been reported

- Amount of credit that has been extended to you
- Other comments or remarks related to an account, such as the fact that you are disputing information related to the account

Inquiries

The inquiries section of your credit report provides the names of creditors and others who have reviewed your credit file for a legally permitted reason. Creditors with whom you have existing accounts may review that information to decide whether to change your terms of credit, increase your credit limit, and so on. Other creditors may review your credit file to decide whether to make you a firm offer of credit, and insurance companies may do the same to determine if they want to make you a firm offer of insurance.

Depending on the credit bureau that prepared your credit record, each inquiry may be preceded by such abbreviations as PRM, AM, and AR. PRM indicates that the inquiry was made for promotional purposes. In other words, the information in your credit file was reviewed or screened for a preapproved credit or insurance offer. AM stands for account monitoring and AR for account review, both of which mean that a creditor reviewed the information in your file, perhaps to determine whether it should increase your credit limit or cancel your credit card.

The only types of inquiries that are reported to businesses when they review your credit record information are those that

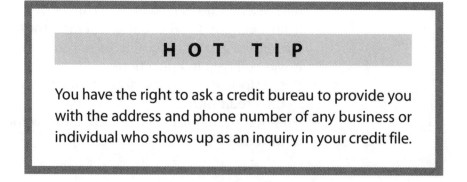

HOT TIP

You have the right to ask a credit bureau to provide you with the address and phone number of any business or individual who shows up as an inquiry in your credit file.

> # WARNING
>
> The inquiries section of your credit report can affect your ability to obtain adequate insurance as well as the cost of your insurance.

result from your application for new or additional credit. In other words, they won't find out about inquiries that were made for promotional or account monitoring purposes.

The FCRA does not specify the maximum amount of time that an inquiry can or should remain in your credit file, but it does require that an inquiry remain in your report for a minimum of two years for employment purposes and a minimum of six months for all other purposes.

At first glance, the inquiries section of your credit report may seem relatively unimportant. However, it can have a significant bearing on your ability to get new or additional credit. That's because when creditors evaluate your request for new or additional credit, one of the factors they will probably consider is the number of inquiries that are the result of your efforts to obtain more credit. If there are a lot of those inquiries, creditors may worry that you are taking on too much debt and will begin having trouble meeting your financial obligations as a result, or that you are already having trouble paying your bills, which is why you are applying for new credit. Either way, they may be less apt to approve your request for new or additional credit, or they may give you that credit but make the terms of the credit relatively expensive.

The FCRA does not give you any rights regarding the inquiries in your credit record. Even so, it is always a good idea to challenge any inquiries that you do not recognize. The credit reporting agency may be willing to investigate them for you,

H O T   T I P

Every time you apply for a credit card, a mortgage loan, a loan from a car financing company, or for some other type of credit, it is likely to show up as an inquiry in your credit record. Therefore, only apply for the credit you really need.

although some credit bureaus will only do so if the inquiries are the result of identity theft.

Public Record Information

This section of your credit report provides information about credit-related problems that are a matter of public record, including bankruptcies, foreclosures, judgments, and tax liens. It will also show if you are behind on a court-ordered child support obligation and if you have been convicted of any crimes.

What Isn't in Your Credit Report

After you receive a copy of your credit report, you may be surprised to discover what isn't being reported. For one thing, since the big three do not get all of their consumer credit record information from the same subscribers, some of your credit accounts may show up in one report and not in another. Also, some subscribers may not report information to credit bureaus every month. For example, some may only report if you default on an account or if an account is sent to collections. Many auto dealers, small department stores and local retailers, utility companies, and medical providers work this way. Figure 2.2 summarizes the reporting patterns of key subscribers.

FIGURE 2.2
Regularly Reported Consumer Account Data

Consumer account data are reported regularly for the following accounts:

- Bank cards

- Large retailers such as Sears and J. C. Penney

- American Express and other travel and entertainment cards

- Airline charge cards

- Mortgages

- Federally guaranteed student loans

In most cases, consumer data on the following accounts is not reported to credit bureaus unless an account is past due, in collections, or a delinquency on an account results in a lawsuit or a judgment against a consumer:

- Utility bills

- Oil and gas cards (Some oil and gas companies report regularly.)

- Medical bills

- Rent payments

- Auto dealer loans

- Credit union loans (Some credit unions report regularly.)

- Accounts with smaller department stores and local retailers

The Scoop on Credit Scores

Creditors are making greater use of credit scores to help them make decisions about consumers who apply for new or additional credit. For example, nearly all mortgages are now underwritten using credit scores. Creditors are also using credit scores to evaluate their existing account holders. Depending on what your score is, your credit limit could be reduced, the rate of interest you are paying could be raised, and other terms of credit could be affected. Insurance companies are also using credit scores more often.

Your credit score is a numeric representation of your creditworthiness. It predicts how you are likely to manage credit in the future based on how you've managed credit in the past. It is calculated by applying a mathematical model to the information in your credit record, including your account payment history, the amount of debt you owe, the length of your credit history, and the kinds of credit you have, among other things. As the information in your credit file changes, so will your credit score.

The main provider of credit scores is a company called Fair Isaac, Inc. It is the creator of the FICO score, which is used by about 70 percent of all financial institutions. However, some companies have developed their own credit scores, and each one may use a slightly different formula, plug somewhat different information into the formula, and/or weigh the information differently, even though they all take consumer credit record data into account.

Each of the three national credit reporting agencies have worked with Fair, Isaac to develop their own credit scores based on the information in their particular databases. Equifax's credit score is known as BEACON, Experian's is the Experian/Fair, Isaac Risk Score, and TransUnion's is called EMPIRICA. Because the information in your credit file will probably vary from credit bureau to credit bureau, your score will vary, too. In fact, a recent study by the Consumer Federation of America and the National Credit Reporting Association showed substantial diffrences among consumer credit scores depending on which national credit bureau a score is ordered from. Therefore, you could get a high score from one credit bureau and a mediocre score from another.

How to Order Your Credit Score

You should order your credit score from each of the national credit bureaus every six months, just like you should review your credit reports every six months.

It's also a good idea to order your credit score as well as a copy of your credit report before you apply for important credit, because the lender may review both. Also, some creditors may review your credit scores from all three credit bureaus. If there are differences, the creditors may either use the middle score or apply a mathematical formula to come up with one score.

To order your credit scores from each of the three national credit bureaus, you can call their toll-free numbers, mail your request to them, or go to their Web sites. Information explaining how to use each option was provided earlier in this chapter.

Until the passage of FACTA, credit reporting agencies were free to set their own fees when they sold consumers their credit scores. Now, however, they FTC must set a standard "fair and

HOT TIP

To order your Fair, Isaac credit score, go to the company's Web site <www.myfico.com>. While you are there, you can also use a Loan Savings Calculator to determine how different FICO scores will affect the cost of a loan you might apply for, and you can get tips for how to improve your score.

reasonable" fee for a credit score when you purchase it from a credit bureau. At the time this book was written, that fee had not been determined, but once it is, it will be available at the author's Web site <www.johnventure.com>. This standard fee will not apply when you purchase your credit score from Fair, Isaac.

Also, when you order your credit score from a credit reporting agency, FACTA requires it to provide you with specific written information. This information includes:

- A statement that your credit score and the model that was used to develop it may be different than the one used by a creditor
- A written explanation of your score and the range of possible scores with the model the credit bureau used
- A summary of up to four key factors that may have adversely affected your credit score (If the number of inquiries in your credit file had an adverse effect on your score, this fact must also be disclosed, unless it is included among the four key factors.)
- The date your score was created
- The name, address, and Web site of the company that created your credit score, if the credit bureau did not create it

What You Can Do to Improve Your Credit Score

The credit scores provided by Equifax, Experian, and TransUnion range from 300 to 850. The higher the score, the better. The lower the score, the greater the penalty you will pay in terms of the interest rate you qualify for when you apply for credit and the other terms of credit you will be offered.

Here are some suggestions for raising your score and keeping it high.

- Pay all of your debts on time.
- Keep your debt levels down. A high debt-to-income ratio works against you.
- Use your credit cards but pay down the balances. Don't let them mount up. Many credit scores compare the amount

H O T   T I P

Under FACTA, when you get a loan from a mortgage lender and secure it with one to four pieces of residential real estate, if the lender used your credit score as part of its decision-making process, it must disclose your credit score to you as soon as is "reasonably practicable." If the lender used a credit score supplied by one of the credit reporting agencies, it must also give you the company's name, address, and phone number, as well as any related information about you that it may have obtained. If the mortgage lender uses an automated underwriting system, it must disclose the credit score that its system generated for you and the key factors that were taken into account to produce the score. In addition, the lender must give you a standardized and specifically worded notice that provides you with general information regarding what a credit score is, how it is generated, how the lender may use it, and so on.

of debt you have to your credit limits. If the amount you owe is close to your limit, your credit score will probably be negatively affected.

- Don't have a lot of credit accounts. Although it is helpful to have some long established credit accounts with a variety of creditors—a national bank card and a bank loan for example—too many credit accounts can lower your credit score.

HOT TIP

The factors that go into calculating your credit score are interrelated. Therefore, if one factor changes, your score may change too, but overall improvement in your score will depend on how each factor relates to all of the other factors that were considered in determining your score. Therefore, if you are turned down for the credit you want because of your credit score, ask the creditor what you can do to improve it.

- Minimize the amount of credit you apply for within a short period of time. Your score may be negatively affected if you have a lot of inquiries in your credit report because you applied for a lot of credit recently. However, inquiries that are the result of account monitoring or prescreened credit offers don't count. Open new credit accounts only if you really need to.
- Get problems in your credit history corrected right away.
- Avoid finance company loans.
- Minimize the frequency with which you transfer balances from one card to another.
- Use exactly the same name on all applications.

3

How to Read Credit Reports from the Three National Credit Bureaus

Mike R. came to see me about rebuilding his credit. Following my advice, he got a copy of his credit report from each of the three national credit bureaus so he could make sure that everything in the reports was accurate.

Several weeks after our first meeting, Mike showed up in my office with his credit reports in hand. He had questions about some of the information, so we sat down and began reviewing them. I pointed out the accounts that would present the biggest problems for him during the rebuilding process, and Mike noticed two negative items that he thought were incorrect. I told Mike that he should get the information corrected.

In this chapter, I help you understand how to read the credit reports produced by Equifax, Experian, and TransUnion. If you read this chapter and are still confused about something in one of your reports, contact the appropriate credit bureau either by calling the number listed on your credit report or by calling the toll-free number provided in the previous chapter. As you learned in Chapter 2, credit bureaus are legally required to have personnel available to help you make sense of your reports.

Systems for Reporting Consumer Information

Although the types of information found in the credit reports of the big three are basically the same, as Chapter 2 explained, the presentation of that information varies somewhat from company to company. Also, each report may vary in regards to the creditor accounts they report on.

Over the past several years, all three of the major credit bureaus have revamped their credit reports to make them more consumer friendly. Now the reports present their information in a clearer, more straightforward manner and they use fewer symbols. Also, if you review your credit report online, it may look different than if it is mailed to you. However, the information in both reports is the same; it's just presented using different formats.

The Equifax Credit Report

Figure 3.1 is a sample of an Equifax credit report ordered through the mail.

FIGURE 3.1
Sample Equifax Credit Report

Note: This is a copy of an actual credit file. Identifying information (e.g., name, address, Social Security number, date of birth, account numbers) has been removed to protect the consumer's identity.

CSC Credit Services

CREDIT FILE

Please address all future correspondence to:
CSC Credit Services
PO Box 981221
El Paso TX 79998
Phone: 1 (888) 501-6254
M - F 9:00am to 5:00pm in your time zone.

FIGURE 3.1

Sample Equifax Credit Report, continued

Please have a copy of this file when calling Consumer Services for assistance. As information is updated regularly, please call us within 60 days from the date of this credit file.

Personal Identification Information   March 29, 2003

Social Security #:

Telephone: (   )

Previous Address(es):

Last Reported Employment:

Previous Employment(s):   U K

Credit Account Information (For your security, the last 4 digits of your account number(s) have been replaced by *)

Company Name	Account Number	Whose Acct	Date Opened	Months Reviewed	Date of Last Activity	High Credit	Terms	Balance	Past Due	Status	Date Reported
American Express CREDIT CARD	*	I	04/75	1	01/03	$1011				01	03/03
American Express CREDIT CARD AMOUNT IN H/C COLUMN IS CREDIT LIMIT	*	I	12/75	1	C3/03	$7000		$4068		R1	03/03
Assoc/Citibank SD PAID ACCOUNT/ZERO BALANCE CLOSED ACCOUNT	4*	I	04/84	24	08/96	$2200		$0		R1	07/98
Assoc/Citibank SD PAID ACCOUNT/ZERO BALANCE CLOSED ACCOUNT	*	I	04/84	19	09/96	$2200		$0		R	07/98
Assoc/Citibank SD PAID ACCOUNT/ZERO BALANCE CLOSED ACCOUNT	*	I	04/84	94	08/97	$2200		$0		R1	12/97
Bank of America REAL ESTATE MORTGAGE		I	01/98	57	09/02	$6171	119	$0		I1	10/02
Bank of America PAID ACCOUNT/ZERO BALANCE HOME IMPROVEMENT LOAN	*	I	06/97		07/97	$4571	76	$0		I0	07/97
Bank One CREDIT CARD AMOUNT IN H/C COLUMN IS CREDIT LIMIT	*	J	11/98	51	02/03	$31700	216	$10806		R1	02/03
Bloomingdale's/Fds	*	I	01/74	99	06/93	$501		$0		R1	03/03
Chase Na CREDIT CARD AMOUNT IN H/C COLUMN IS CREDIT LIMIT	*	I	04/84	45	02/03	$5800	25	$1251		R1	02/03
Chase Na ACCOUNT CLOSED AT CONSUMER'S REQUEST PAID ACCOUNT/ZERO BALANCE		I	04/84	44	03/02	$3000		$0		R1	02/03
Chevron USA CREDIT CARD	*	I	09/66	99	02/03	$445	20	$338		R1	02/03
Citi Cards Cbsdna ACCOUNT CLOSED BY CONSUMER AMOUNT IN H/C COLUMN IS CREDIT LIMIT		I	12/99	12	09/00	$10000		$0		R1	12/00

(Continued on reverse)

FIGURE 3.1

Sample Equifax Credit Report, continued

Credit Account Information - Continued

Company Name / Account Number	Whose Acct	Date Opened	Months Reviewed	Date of Last Activity	High Credit	Terms	Balance	Past Due	Status	Date Reported
First USA *	J	09/96	35	08/99	$3000		$0		R1	10/02
ACCOUNT CLOSED AT CONSUMER'S REQUEST PAID ACCOUNT/ZERO BALANCE										
First USA Na *	A	09/02	6	03/03	$6000	80	$4024		R1	03/03
CREDIT CARD AMOUNT IN H/C COLUMN IS CREDIT LIMIT										
Foleys *	I	07/01	20	08/01	$73		$0		R1	03/03
CHARGE										
Frost National Ban *	J	11/01	14	02/03	$4929	99	$4929		I1	02/03
Frost National Ban *	J	04/01	21	09/02	$5000	166	$0		I1	02/03
Frost National Ban *	J	04/94	99	02/03	$14436	137	$7619		I1	02/03
Frost National Ban *	T	08/98	31	01/01	$8000	141	$0		I1	04/01
PAID ACCOUNT/ZERO BALANCE										
Frost National Ban *	J	08/94	46	06/97	$5000	163	$0		I1	07/98
PAID ACCOUNT/ZERO BALANCE										
Frost National Ban *	J	07/93	15	11/93	$25000	231	$0		I1	11/94
M.B.N.A Amer *	I	12/98	47	11/02	$10000		$0		R1	11/02
Previous Payment History: 1 Time 30 days late Previous Status: 04/01 - R2 ACCOUNT CLOSED BY CONSUMER CREDIT CARD										
Address:										
Norwest Card Servi *	I	05/98	26	07/00	$5000		$0		R1	07/00
ACCOUNT CLOSED AT CONSUMER'S REQUEST CREDIT CARD										
Universal Card/Cbs *	I	02/03			$8000		$0		R1	02/03
CREDIT CARD AMOUNT IN H/C COLUMN IS CREDIT LIMIT										
Wells FARGO Bank T *	I	08/01	17	03/03	$0	153	$7850		I1	03/03
Wells FARGO Bank T *	I	07/00	13	08/01	$5000	106	$0		I1	09/01
PAID ACCOUNT/ZERO BALANCE										
Wells FARGO Bank T *	I	09/97	8	01/98	$40000	9999	$0		I3	05/98
Previous Payment History: 2 Times 30 days late; 1 Time 60 days late; 1 Time 90 + days late Previous Status: 03/98 - I3; 02/98 - I2 PAID ACCOUNT/ZERO BALANCE SECURED										
Address:										
Wells FARGO Bank T *	I	06/97	3	10/97	$40000	3M			I1	10/97
Wells FARGO Bank T *	S	03/81	46	01/97	$30500	352	$0		I1	01/97
PAID ACCOUNT/ZERO BALANCE REAL ESTATE MORTGAGE										
Wells FARGO Card S *	I	04/84	99	05/94	$3000		$0		R1	04/95
Wells FARGO Home M *	J	02/02	11	03/03	$109K	1801	$99334		I1	03/03
REAL ESTATE MORTGAGE										
Wells FARGO Home M *	I	03/98	58	03/03	$67750	1015	$51452		I1	03/03
REAL ESTATE MORTGAGE										
Wells FARGO Home M *	J	03/81	12	03/98	$30500	365	$0		I1	04/98
PAID ACCOUNT/ZERO BALANCE REAL ESTATE MORTGAGE										

FIGURE 3.1
Sample Equifax Credit Report, continued

CSC Credit Services

CREDIT FILE

Date: March 29, 2003

Companies that Requested your Credit File

03/29/03 Equifax - Disclosure	03/25/03 Equifax - Disclosure
03/06/03 Rels Reporting Services WF HOME MTG-8024 AUS	02/06/03 PRM-Direct Lending Source Inc
01/08/03 PRM-First USA Bank	01/06/03 PRM-At&T Wireless
12/20/02 PRM-First USA Bank	12/18/02 PRM-Capital One,FSB
12/17/02 PRM-First USA Bank	12/11/02 PRM-First USA Bank
12/09/02 PRM-First USA Bank	11/27/02 PRM-First North American National
11/20/02 AR-MBNA	11/18/02 PRM-First USA Bank
10/14/02 AR-Wells FARGO Home Mortgage	10/14/02 PRM-Western SIERRA Acceptance
10/11/02 AR-Wells FARGO Home Mortgage Inc	09/16/02 PRM-Capital One
09/09/02 PRM-Capital One,FSB	09/06/02 PRM-At&T Wireless
08/26/02 PRM-Household Bank	08/26/02 AR-MBNA
08/16/02 PRM-Blair Corporation	08/07/02 AR-Chevron USA
07/26/02 PRM-At&T Wireless	07/23/02 AR-MBNA
07/11/02 PRM-Universal Card / Cbsdna	07/11/02 PRM-Citi Cards Cbsdna
06/26/02 PRM-Shell/Citibank SD	06/21/02 AR-MBNA
06/11/02 PRM-Compass Bank	06/10/02 PRM-Universal Card / Cbsdna
06/10/02 PRM-Citi Cards Cbsdna	05/23/02 Working Assets
05/22/02 AR-MBNA	05/09/02 PRM-Citifinancial
05/02/02 PRM-Direct Lending Source Inc	05/01/02 PRM-Household Bank
04/22/02 AR-MBNA	04/18/02 AR-Wells FARGO Home Mortgage Inc
04/10/02 PRM-At&T Wireless	04/04/02 PRM-Household Bank
04/02/02 AR-Federal Home Loan Mortgage Crp	11/28/01 Rels Reporting Services WF HOME MTG8024 AUST
11/14/01 Frost Bank Lending	04/13/01 Frost Bank Lending

Source: Reprinted by permission of Equifax, Inc.

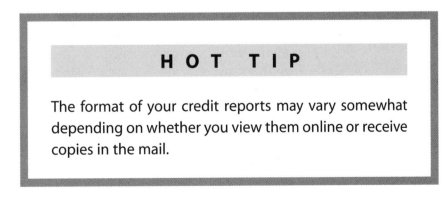

HOT TIP

The format of your credit reports may vary somewhat depending on whether you view them online or receive copies in the mail.

Personal Identification Information

This first section of the Equifax report indicates your name and address and may also list one or more previous addresses, depending on how long you have been living at your current address. It also lists your Social Security number, phone number, date of birth, and last reported employment.

Public Record Information

This next section of the Equifax report presents public record information pulled from local, state, and federal court records. The sample credit report in Figure 3.1 includes no public record information. However, it could include information on liens filed against your property, details on any bankruptcies you may have filed, and information about any judgments an individual or business may have won against you as a result of a lawsuit, among other things.

Lien information will include the date the lien was filed and where it was filed, the case or ID number related to the lien, the amount of the lien, whether it was released, and the release date.

Bankruptcy-related information will include the date the bankruptcy was filed, the federal district court it was filed in, the case or ID number, the total dollar amount of assets and liabilities involved in the bankruptcy, and whether the bankruptcy was discharged at the time of the report.

Judgment information will include the date a judgment was filed in a lawsuit, the case number or other identifying number, the names of the lawsuit defendant and plaintiff, the amount of the judgment, whether it was satisfied (paid), and the date it was satisfied.

Collection Agency Account Information

This section of the Equifax report notes any accounts that may have been turned over to a collection agency. The sample report includes no collection account information, but if it did, the information would appear immediately after the Public Record Information and before the Credit Account Information section of your report.

If any collection accounts are in your report, the following information will be provided for each account:

- The date the collection account was reported
- The date the account was assigned to a collection agency and the name and phone number of the collection agency
- The name of the creditor who turned the account over to a collection agency
- The dollar amount that is in collection
- The status of the collection effort—if any money has been paid on the collection account and the date of the last activity on the account, for example
- The type of account (e.g., individual, joint) and the account number

Credit Account Information

The section of the report labeled Credit Account Information lists open and closed accounts that are reported to Equifax. Under this major heading is a series of subheadings. Moving from left to right, the first subheading is Company Name. The names of the creditors who reported to Equifax are listed under this heading, and to the right of each creditor name is an account number.

To the right of those account numbers is a series of narrow columns with separate headings, and under those headings is specific information related to each of the accounts. A brief explanation of the information in these columns follows.

Whose Account

Equifax uses nine different letter codes to indicate who is responsible for an account, e.g., I (individual), J (joint), S (shared), and so on. Your Equifax credit report will come with explanations for each of the nine letter codes.

Date Opened

Date Opened indicates the month and year an account was opened.

Months Reviewed and Date of Last Activity

Months Reviewed refers to the number of months of payment history reported to Equifax for an account. On the sample report, those numbers range from 1 month to 99 months.

Date of Last Activity is the last date for which there was any activity on an account. The activity could represent the last time you made a payment on an account or the last time you charged something on the account.

High Credit and Terms

High Credit indicates either the maximum amount you have ever charged to an account or an account's credit limit.

Terms indicate either the number of installment payments for a revolving account or the amount of the monthly payment for an installment account.

Items as of Date Reported

This subheading contains three columns of information. The column labeled Balance refers to the amount owed on an account at the time that the creditor reported it to Equifax. The Past Due column indicates how much money, if any, was past due at the time the account information was reported.

Two kinds of information are represented by the letter/number codes found in the column labeled Status. The letter part of each code indicates the type of account being reported. *O* refers to an open account, one in which the entire balance is due each month. *R* refers to a revolving account—the monthly payment amount will depend on the account balance. *I* signifies an installment account, one with a fixed number of payments.

The number part of the code provides information about the timeliness of the payments on an account. For example, a 1 indicates that the account payments have been made as agreed and that the account is in good standing, a 2 means that the account is 30 days or more past due, and a 7 signifies that regular payments are being made under a wage earner plan, also known as a Chapter 13 bankruptcy. There are six other numbers, each of which is defined in the information that will come with your Equifax credit report.

Date Reported

The Date Reported information indicates when information on an account was last reported to Equifax. It appears in the column to the far right of the credit history section of the Equifax report.

Other Account Information

Other information is provided in the Credit Account Information section of the Equifax credit report. For example, there is information regarding the prior payment history on some accounts—in the sample report, for the MBNA America credit account and Wells Fargo Bank. Previous payment history information tells how frequently a consumer was 30, 60, or 90 days late with an account payment during the months for which account information was provided. For example, in the case of the MBNA account on the sample report, the consumer was 30 days late one time. Other data that might appear in this section of a Equifax report includes whether a consumer or a creditor closed an account and whether an account was transferred or sold.

Companies That Requested Your Credit File

At the end of the Equifax report is a list of the businesses that reviewed the information in the sample credit file during the previous 24 months and the date of each review. This section is generally referred to as the Inquiries section of a credit report. As you will notice from the sample report, a letter code precedes some the business names in this section of the Equifax report. The sample report shows two codes: PRM and AR. PRM represents a promotional inquiry. If you see these three letters next to the names of any creditors in the Inquiries section of your report, it means that Equifax gave them your name and address so they could offer you credit. If AM or AR appears next to a creditor's name, it means that the creditor made a periodic review of your credit history, maybe to decide whether to change the terms of your credit or to raise or lower your credit limit.

The Experian Credit Report

A sample of the online version of Experian's credit report is shown in Figure 3.2. The report comes with an investigation request form. If you order your report by mail or by phone, your report will look slightly different than the online report, but the information will be the same.

Report Number

Each Experian credit report has a Report Number. It appears in the upper left corner of the sample report. Use this number if you contact Experian via phone, letter, or online about your credit report.

Credit History

Accounts with adverse information are listed first in the Experian report. Negative public record information will also appear here. There is no negative information in the sample report. The creditors in this section of the report are listed in alphabetical order together with their addresses and account numbers. Below each account is information about its status—the number of months the account is past due, whether the creditor

FIGURE 3.2
Sample Experian Credit Report

Sample Credit Report   Page 1 of 3

Report Number ❶
2818573907

Personal Credit Report from Experian for
John Q. Consumer

Report Date: 04/12/00

Index:
- Potentially Negative Items
- Accounts in Good Standing
- Requests for Your Credit History
- Personal Information
- Your Personal Statement(s)

Go Back

❷

Report number:
You will need your report number to contact Experian online, by phone or by mail.

Potentially Negative Items ❸   back to top

Index:
Navigate through the sections of your credit report using these links.

Credit Items

BNBUSA/COMPUSA

Address:	Account Number:
P O BOX 15519	7001306000461...
WILMINGTON, DE 19850	

Status:
open/past due 30 days. $20 past due as of 8-1998.

Status Details:
As of 6-2005, this account is scheduled to go to a positive status.

Date Opened:	Type:	Credit Limit/Original Amount:
10/1997	Revolving	$3000
Reported Since:	Terms:	High Balance:
10/1997	NA	$3193
Date of Status:	Monthly Payment:	Recent Balance:
08/1998	10	$0as of 08/30/1998
Last Reported:	Responsibility:	Recent Payment:
08/1998	Individual	3193

Potentially negative items:
Items that creditors may view negatively. It includes the creditor's name and address, your account number (shortened for security), account status, type and terms of the account and any other information reported to Experian by the creditor. Also includes any bankruptcy, lien and judgment information obtained directly from the courts.

CHEVY CHASE FED SAV BANK

Address:	Account Number:
6202 PRESIDENTS COURT	5407301009607...
FREDERICK, MD 21701	

Status:
open/past due 60 days. $96 past due as of 8-1998.

Status Details:
As of 7-2005, this account is scheduled to go to a positive status.

Date Opened:	Type:	Credit Limit/Original Amount:
11/1995	Revolving	$1500
Reported Since:	Terms:	High Balance:
12/1995	NA	$1798
Date of Status:	Monthly Payment:	Recent Balance:
08/1998	131	$0 as of 08/15/1998
Last Reported:	Responsibility:	Recent Payment:
08/1998	Joint	1798

Status details:
Indicates when information will be removed from your credit history.

CITIBANK PREFERRED VISA

Address:	Account Number:
P O BOX 6500	4271382104687...
SIOUX FALLS, SD 57117	

Status:
account charged off/past due 150 days. $8,486 written off in 8-1998. $1,538 past due as of 8-1998.

Status Details: ❹
This account is scheduled to continue on record until 1-2005.

Date Opened:	Type:	Credit Limit/Original Amount:
01/1997	Revolving	$8000
Reported Since:	Terms:	High Balance:
01/1997	NA	$8486
Date of Status:	Monthly Payment:	Recent Balance:
05/1998	0	$0 as of 08/30/1998
Last Reported:	Responsibility:	Recent Payment:
08/1998	Individual	8486

Account History:
Between 3-1998 and 4-1998, your credit limit/high balance was $8,000

Balance History:
$8337 04/1998
$8171 03/1998

If you believe information in your report is inaccurate, you can dispute that item quickly, effectively and cost free by using Experian's online dispute service located at:

experian.com/yourcredit

Disputing online is the fastest way to address any concern you may have about the information in your credit report.

(continued)

FIGURE 3.2
Sample Experian Credit Report, continued

Sample Credit Report   Page 2 of 3

Accounts in Good Standing   **5**   back to top

BB & B

Address:	Account Number:
2035 WEST 4TH STREET	138300759...
TEMPE, AZ 85281	

Status: Status Details:
open/never late.

Date Opened:	Type: **6**	Credit Limit/Original Amount:
10/1997	Revolving	NA
Reported Since:	Terms:	High Balance:
10/1997	NA	$Unknown
Date of Status:	Monthly Payment:	Recent Balance:
10/1997	0	$0/paid as of 12/1997
Last Reported:	Responsibility:	Recent Payment:
12/1997	Individual	0

MACYS NJ NY

Address:	Account Number:
9111 DUKE BLVD	335646403...
MASON, OH 45040	

Status: Status Details:
closed/never late.   This account is scheduled to continue on record until 4-2005.

Date Opened:	Type:	Credit Limit/Original Amount:
09/1994	Revolving	$500
Reported Since:	Terms:	High Balance:
02/1996	NA	$75
Date of Status:	Monthly Payment:	Recent Balance:
04/1998	5	$0 as of 04/1998
Last Reported:	Responsibility:	Recent Payment:
04/1998	Individual	75

Creditor's statement regarding this item: Account closed at
credit grantor's request.

Requests for Your Credit History   **7**   back to top

MBNA AMERICA/CREDIT

Address:	Date of Request:
400 CHRISTIANA RD MS7009	09/1998
NEWARK, DE 19713	

CITIBANK

Address:	Date of Request:
670 MASON RDGE CTR MS761	03/1998
SAINT LOUIS, MO 63141	

ADVANTA NATIONAL BANK

Address:	Date of Request:
650 NAAMANS ROAD	12/1997
CLAYMONT, DE 19703	

PROVIDIAN BANCORP

Address:	Date of Request:
PO BOX 9120	05/1997
PLEASANTON, CA 94566	

*Accounts in good
standing:*

Lists accounts that have a
positive status and may be
viewed favorably by
creditors. Some creditors
do not report to us, so some
of your accounts may not be
listed.

Type:

Account type indicates
whether your account is a
revolving or an installment
account.

Requests for your credit history:

Also called "inquiries", requests for your credit
history are logged on your report whenever
anyone reviews your credit information. There
are two types of inquiries.

i.
Inquiries resulting from a transaction initiated by
you. These include inquiries from your
applications for credit, insurance, housing or
other loans. They also include transfer of an
account to a collection agency. Creditors may
view these items when evaluating your
creditworthiness.

ii.
Inquiries resulting from transactions you may not
have initiated but that are allowed under the
FCRA. These include preapproved offers, as well
as for employment, investment review, account
monitoring by existing creditors, and requests by
you for your own report. These items are shown
only to you and have no impact on your
creditworthiness or risk scores.

FIGURE 3.2
Sample Experian Credit Report, continued

Sample Credit Report   Page 3 of 3

Personal Information   8   back to top

For your protection, the Social Security number you used to obtain this report is not displayed.

Names:
John Q. Consumer
Jonathon Q. Consumer
J.Q. Consumer

Social Security Number Variations:
999999999

Date of Birth:
09/03/1954

Spouse's First Name:
Jane

Employers:
DEBAJ ENGINEERING CORP

Address: 123 MAIN STREET
ANYTOWN, MD 90001-9999
Type of Residence: Multifamily
Geographical Code: 0-156510-31-8840

Address: 13415 BUCHANAN DR   9
FORT WASHINGTON, MD20744-2932
Type of Residence: Single family
Geographical Code: 0-176510-33-8840

Address: 8604 2ND AVE #163
SILVER SPRING, MD20910-3380
Type of Residence: Apartment complex
Geographical Code: 0-156510-31-8840

Notices:
This address is a non-residential address: 8604 2ND AVE SILVER SPRING MD 20910.   10
COMMERCIAL BUSINESS ADDRESS: 8604 2ND AVE, SILVER SPRING, MD, 20910.

Your Personal Statement(s)   back to top

There are no general personal statements currently displaying on your personal credit report   11

Contacting Us   back to top

Contact address and phone number for your area will display here

End of Report

Personal information:

Personal information associated with your history that has been reported to Experian by you, your creditors and other sources.

May include name and Social Security number variations, employers, telephone numbers, etc. Experian lists all variations so you know what is being reported to us as belonging to you.

Address information:

Your current address and previous address(es)

Notices:

As part of Experian's fraud prevention program, any notices with additional information may appear in this section.

Personal statement:

Any personal statement that you added to your report appears here. Note - statements added remain part of the report for 2 years and display to anyone who has permission to review your report.

Source: Reprinted by permission of Experian.

has written off the account for nonpayment, and so on. This section of the report also provides other details on the status of the account—how much longer negative information about an account will continue to be reported by Experian, for example.

Below the Status information are details such as the date the account was opened, the type of the account, who is responsible for paying the account, the account credit limit, and the account's high balance and recent balance. Next in the Experian credit report comes information about accounts that are in good standing.

Requests for Your Credit History

This section of the Experian credit report is equivalent to the Inquiries section in other credit reports. The inquiries are listed chronologically, from most recent to oldest.

Personal Information

Following the Requests for Your Credit History section of the Experian report is the Personal Information section. This provides the name, Social Security number, date of birth, current and past addresses for the consumer, first name of consumer's spouse, and the name/s of the consumer's employer/s. Any written statements in the consumer's credit record will appear next, followed by a name and phone number for contacting Experian.

The TransUnion Credit Report

Figure 3.3 is a sample TransUnion credit report. The TransUnion report comes with an investigation request form for disputing information in your credit report.

Identifying Information

Your name, Social Security number, current address and former addresses, birth date, and phone number will appear close to the top of your TransUnion credit report. The names and locations of your current and former employers will also appear in this section of the report together with your job titles.

FIGURE 3.3
Sample TransUnion Credit Report

```
P.O. BOX 1000                  YOUR TRANS UNION FILE NUMBER: 100AA1049-001
CHESTER, PA 19022-1000         PAGE  1 OF  4 (INTL USE: DR Z5251 06CH 03)
                               DATE THIS REPORT PRINTED: 04/03/2000
RETURN SERVICE REQUESTED
                               SOCIAL SECURITY NUMBER: 222-22-2222
                               BIRTH DATE:           04/1965
                               YOU HAVE BEEN IN OUR FILES SINCE: 08/1978
                               AKA: CONSUMER,WILLIAM
                               PHONE: 555-5555


CONSUMER REPORT FOR:


    *****
    CONSUMER, BILL
    987 N MAIN ST
    CHICAGO, IL 60606


FORMER ADDRESSES REPORTED:

  12123 PAXSON CT, CHICAGO, IL 60605
  11111 JORDAN DR, CHICAGO, IL 60623

EMPLOYMENT DATA REPORTED:

  ABC CARDBOARD COMPANY           IHOP
  CHICAGO, IL                     CHICAGO, IL
  POSITION: MANAGER               POSITION: CHEF
  DATE VERIFIED: 04/1993          DATE REPORTED: 01/1990

               YOUR CREDIT INFORMATION
```
```
THE FOLLOWING ITEMS OBTAINED FROM PUBLIC RECORDS APPEAR ON YOUR REPORT. YOU MAY
BE REQUIRED TO EXPLAIN PUBLIC RECORD ITEMS TO POTENTIAL CREDITORS.  ANY BANK-
RUPTCY INFORMATION WILL REMAIN ON YOUR REPORT FOR 10 YEARS FROM THE DATE OF
FILING.  UNPAID TAX LIENS ARE REPORTED INDEFINITELY.  ALL OTHER PUBLIC RECORD
INFORMATION, INCLUDING DISCHARGED CHAPTER 13 BANKRUPTCY AND ANY ACCOUNTS
CONTAINING ADVERSE INFORMATION, REMAIN FOR 7 YEARS.

DOCKET #14550035     MUNICIPAL COURT     CIVIL JUDGMENT
PLAINTIFF:           CNA INSURANCE COMPANY          ENTERED:  10/1997
PLAINTIFF ATTORNEY: TROY MCCLURE                    AMOUNT:    $5000

DOCKET #4024234      RECORDER OF DEEDS    RELEASE OF TAX LIEN
PLAINTIFF:           WATERFORD COUNTY               ENTERED:  01/1998
PLAINTIFF ATTORNEY: SAM WATERSON                    AMOUNT:     $683
                                                    PAID:     06/1998

DOCKET #SV4348447    FEDERAL DISTRICT     CHAPTER 13 BANKRUPTCY DISCHARGED
PLAINTIFF ATTORNEY: HEIDI YOUNG                     ENTERED:  07/1999
                                    ASSETS:    $0   PAID:     11/1999
                                                    LIAB:       $0
```
```
THE FOLLOWING ACCOUNTS CONTAIN INFORMATION WHICH SOME CREDITORS MAY CONSIDER TO
BE ADVERSE.  THE ADVERSE INFORMATION IN THESE ACCOUNTS HAS BEEN PRINTED IN
>BRACKETS< FOR YOUR CONVENIENCE, TO HELP YOU UNDERSTAND YOUR REPORT.  THEY ARE
NOT BRACKETED THIS WAY FOR CREDITORS. (NOTE: THE ACCOUNT # MAY BE SCRAMBLED BY
THE CREDITOR FOR YOUR PROTECTION).

                                        00411     385  1/8
```

(continued)

FIGURE 3.3
Sample TransUnion Credit Report, continued

```
REPORT ON CONSUMER, BILL                                    PAGE  2 OF  4
SOCIAL SECURITY NUMBER: 222-22-2222     TRANS UNION FILE NUMBER: 100AA1049-001


>COLLECTION RECORD<
  COMMRCL FIN              # 5435355A1           OPEN ACCOUNT
>PLACED FOR COLLECTION<
      UPDATED   12/1999   BALANCE:      $7218    INDIVIDUAL ACCOUNT
      PLACED    11/1999   MOST OWED:    $8154    MBNA BANK
      CLOSED    03/1997  >PAST DUE:       $0<
     >STATUS AS OF 03/1997: COLLECTION ACCOUNT<

  PROVIDIAN                # 4758357375775775    REVOLVING ACCOUNT
  CANCELLED BY CREDIT GRANTOR                    SECURED CREDIT CARD
      UPDATED   02/2000   BALANCE:       $116    INDIVIDUAL ACCOUNT
      OPENED    02/1993   MOST OWED:    $2002
      CLOSED    12/1999  >PAST DUE:      $116<
     >STATUS AS OF 02/2000: CHARGED OFF AS BAD DEBT<

  FRD MOTOR CR             # ECA3323YH6          INSTALLMENT ACCOUNT
                                                 AUTO LEASE
      UPDATED   02/2000   BALANCE:     $17576    INDIVIDUAL ACCOUNT
      OPENED    02/1999   MOST OWED:   $24336    PAY TERMS: 36 MONTHLY $676
                         >PAST DUE:    $1352<
     >STATUS AS OF 02/2000: 60 DAYS PAST DUE<
     >IN PRIOR  8 MONTHS FROM LAST UPDATE  1 TIME 90 DAYS LATE<
     >MAXIMUM DELINQUENCY OF  90 DAYS OCCURRED IN  09/1999<

  AFFORDAL FCU             # 56464               INSTALLMENT ACCOUNT
                                                 INSTALLMENT SALES CONTRACT
      UPDATED   02/2000   BALANCE:        $98    INDIVIDUAL ACCOUNT
      OPENED    06/1999   MOST OWED:     $588    PAY TERMS: 12 MONTHLY $49
                         >PAST DUE:       $98<
     >STATUS AS OF 02/2000: 60 DAYS PAST DUE<
     >IN PRIOR  8 MONTHS FROM LAST UPDATE  1 TIME 90 DAYS LATE<
     >MAXIMUM DELINQUENCY OF  90 DAYS OCCURRED IN  02/2000<

  CHRYS FIN CP             # 6659992218          INSTALLMENT ACCOUNT
  CLOSED                                         AUTOMOBILE
      UPDATED   03/2000   BALANCE:         $0    INDIVIDUAL ACCOUNT
      OPENED    09/1994   MOST OWED:   $36000    PAY TERMS: 60 MONTHLY
      CLOSED    03/2000
      STATUS AS OF 03/2000: PAID OR PAYING AS AGREED
     >IN PRIOR 19 MONTHS FROM DATE CLOSED  2 TIMES 120 DAYS,
      3 TIMES 90 DAYS,  3 TIMES 60 DAYS,  5 TIMES 30 DAYS LATE<
     >MAXIMUM DELINQUENCY OF 120+ DAYS OCCURRED IN 11/1995<

  THE FOLLOWING ITEM IS SUPPRESSED PENDING CREDIT GRANTOR UPDATE:
  SEARS                    # 55453425678         LINE OF CREDIT ACCOUNT
                                                 CREDIT LINE SECURED
      UPDATED   10/1998   BALANCE:       $182    AUTHORIZED ACCOUNT
      OPENED    11/1993   MOST OWED:     $300    PAY TERMS:  MONTHLY $10
                                                 CREDIT LIMIT:      $300
      STATUS AS OF 10/1998: PAID OR PAYING AS AGREED
     >IN PRIOR 48 MONTHS FROM LAST UPDATE  3 TIMES  60 DAYS,
      8 TIMES 30 DAYS LATE<
     >MAXIMUM DELINQUENCY OF  60 DAYS OCCURRED IN  08/1996<


                                               00411    386  2/8
```

FIGURE 3.3
Sample TransUnion Credit Report, continued

```
REPORT ON CONSUMER, BILL                               PAGE  3 OF  4
SOCIAL SECURITY NUMBER: 222-22-2222     TRANS UNION FILE NUMBER: 100AA1049-001


  JCPENNY                  # 5558353589559      REVOLVING ACCOUNT
                                                CHARGE ACCOUNT
     UPDATED  03/2000   BALANCE:        $177    INDIVIDUAL ACCOUNT
     OPENED   10/1994   MOST OWED:       $354   PAY TERMS:  MINIMUM $15
                        >PAST DUE:        $30<
     >STATUS AS OF 03/2000: 30 DAYS PAST DUE<
     >IN PRIOR 48 MONTHS FROM LAST UPDATE  1 TIME   90 DAYS,
      3 TIMES 60 DAYS,  8 TIMES 30 DAYS LATE<
     >MAXIMUM DELINQUENCY OF   90 DAYS OCCURRED IN  02/1998<

  CAPITAL 1 BK             # 4121741407602009   REVOLVING ACCOUNT
  CANCELLED BY CREDIT GRANTOR                   CREDIT CARD
     UPDATED  03/2000   BALANCE:        $243    INDIVIDUAL ACCOUNT
     OPENED   11/1994   MOST OWED:      $1577   PAY TERMS:  MINIMUM $40
                        >PAST DUE:       $243<
     >STATUS AS OF 03/2000: 120 DAYS PAST DUE<
     >IN PRIOR 17 MONTHS FROM LAST UPDATE  2 TIMES 120 DAYS,
      1 TIME  90 DAYS,  1 TIME  60 DAYS,  1 TIME  30 DAYS LATE<
     >MAXIMUM DELINQUENCY OF 120+ DAYS OCCURRED IN 07/1999<


  THE FOLLOWING ACCOUNTS ARE REPORTED WITH NO ADVERSE INFORMATION

  LOAN SVCE CT             # 2424004244226      INSTALLMENT ACCOUNT
                                                STUDENT LOAN
     UPDATED  01/2000   BALANCE:       $5550    INDIVIDUAL ACCOUNT
     OPENED   09/1999   MOST OWED:      $5946   PAY TERMS: 60  MONTHLY $99
     STATUS AS OF 01/2000: PAID OR PAYING AS AGREED
     IN PRIOR  4 MONTHS FROM LAST UPDATE NEVER LATE


  MILEAGE PLUS             # 4584854873765      REVOLVING ACCOUNT
                                                CREDIT CARD
     UPDATED  03/2000   BALANCE:       $8037    INDIVIDUAL ACCOUNT
     OPENED   03/1998   MOST OWED:      $9000   PAY TERMS:  MINIMUM $160
                                                CREDIT LIMIT:      $9000
     STATUS AS OF 03/2000: PAID OR PAYING AS AGREED
     IN PRIOR 24 MONTHS FROM LAST UPDATE NEVER LATE


  THE FOLLOWING COMPANIES HAVE RECEIVED YOUR CREDIT REPORT.  THEIR INQUIRIES
  REMAIN ON YOUR CREDIT REPORT FOR TWO YEARS. (NOTE: "TU CONSUMER DISCLOSURE"
  INQUIRIES ARE NOT VIEWED BY CREDITORS).

  INQUIRY TYPE  DATE         SUBSCRIBER NAME
  INDIVIDUAL    03/09/2000   FDR/FIRST SUBURBAN MTG
     PERMISSIBLE PURPOSE = CONSUMER INITIATED TRANSACTION
  INDIVIDUAL    02/26/2000   CONSUMER INS SVC/RELIANT
     PERMISSIBLE PURPOSE = INSURANCE UNDERWRITING
  INDIVIDUAL    01/24/2000   TU CONSUMER DISCLOSURE
  INDIVIDUAL    11/04/1999   FIRST SUBURBAN MORTG VIA FINANCIAL DATA RPTS
     PERMISSIBLE PURPOSE = CONSUMER INITIATED TRANSACTION
  INDIVIDUAL    10/14/1999   VALLEY BELL CR UN
  INDIVIDUAL    10/13/1999   AMERICAN CREDIT EDUCATOR
  INDIVIDUAL    10/13/1999   CITIFINANCIAL
  JOINT         05/26/1999   MORTGAGE EXCHANGE
  INDIVIDUAL    03/22/1999   VALLEY BELL CR UN

                                           00411     387  3/8
```

(continued)

FIGURE 3.3
Sample TransUnion Credit Report, continued

```
REPORT ON CONSUMER, BILL                                  PAGE  4 OF  4
SOCIAL SECURITY NUMBER: 222-22-2222   TRANS UNION FILE NUMBER: 100AA1049-001
```

```
THE COMPANIES LISTED BELOW RECEIVED YOUR NAME, ADDRESS AND OTHER LIMITED
INFORMATION ABOUT YOU SO THEY COULD MAKE A FIRM OFFER OF CREDIT OR INSURANCE.
THEY DID NOT RECEIVE YOUR FULL CREDIT REPORT, AND THESE INQUIRIES ARE NOT SEEN
BY ANYONE BUT YOU.
```

DATE	SUBSCRIBER NAME	DATE	SUBSCRIBER NAME
02/2000	CAPITAL ONE BANK	11/1999	CREDICORP INC
10/1999	FIRST USA DBA BANK ONE	10/1999	CAPITAL ONE BANK
09/1999	CAPITAL ONE BANK	08/1999	PROVIDIAN BANCORP
06/1999	GEICO	04/1999	CONSECO FINANCIAL
01/1999	FIRST CONSUMERS NATIONAL		

```
THE FOLLOWING COMPANIES OBTAINED INFORMATION FROM YOUR CONSUMER REPORT FOR THE
PURPOSE OF AN ACCOUNT REVIEW OR OTHER BUSINESS TRANSACTION WITH YOU. THESE
INQUIRIES ARE NOT DISPLAYED TO ANYONE BUT YOU AND WILL NEVER AFFECT ANY CREDIT
DECISION.
```

DATE	SUBSCRIBER NAME
01/2000	SEARS CARD CYCLES 02/16
12/1999	PREMIER INSURANCE GROUP
	PERMISSIBLE PURPOSE = INSURANCE UNDERWRITING
12/1999	CAPITAL ONE BANK
11/1999	CAPITAL ONE BANK
09/1999	CAPITAL ONE BANK
07/1999	CAPITAL ONE BANK
06/1999	CAPITAL ONE BANK
02/1999	FIRST USA DBA BANK ONE

```
CONSUMER STATEMENT:
     DO NOT CONFUSE WITH CONSUMERS OF SIMILAR IDENTIFICATION; VERIFY
     ALL IDENTIFYING INFORMATION.
```

```
SPECIAL MESSAGES:
     INPUT SSN HAS BEEN USED (003) TIMES IN THE LAST (30) DAYS ON DIFFERENT
     INQUIRIES
```

```
IF YOU BELIEVE ANY OF THE INFORMATION IN YOUR CREDIT REPORT IS INCORRECT,
PLEASE LET US KNOW.  FOR YOUR CONVENIENCE, AN INVESTIGATION FORM IS INCLUDED.
PLEASE COMPLETE IT AND MAIL TO:

TRANS UNION CONSUMER RELATIONS
P.O. BOX 2000
CHESTER, PA 19022-2000

1-800-555-5555
OUR BUSINESS HOURS IN YOUR TIME ZONE ARE:
8:30 A.M. TO 4:30 P.M.
MONDAY THRU FRIDAY
```

```
                                          00411     388   4/8
```

Source: Reprinted by permission of TransUnion.

Public Record Information

The credit information section of the TransUnion report begins with information related to any public record data that may be in your report. In the sample report, there is information about a civil judgment that was entered against the consumer, the release of a tax lien, and the discharge of a Chapter 13 reorganization bankruptcy.

Account Information

Information on the credit accounts that are being reported to TransUnion comes next in the TransUnion credit report, starting with accounts that contain information that creditors may view as negative. The arrowed brackets indicate adverse information. The sample credit record contains a lot of negative information. For example, one account in the sample report was sent to collections, and another account was closed by a creditor.

The names of each of the creditors reporting account information to TransUnion appear on the far left side of the credit report. To the right of this information is an account number for each creditor, and to the right of that is a block of information that indicates the type of account—revolving, installment, line of credit; the type of credit—secured or unsecured credit card, auto loan, student loan, and so on; whether the account is individual or joint or whether the consumer is an authorized user on the account; and the terms of payment for the account.

On the left side of the TransUnion credit report, under the name of each creditor, is the date that the account information was last updated and the balance on the account at that time. Below this information is the date that the account was opened, the most that has been owed on the account, and the amount of money, if any, that is past due on the account.

Moving down the page and reading from left to right, there is information about the status of the account at the time information was reported. On the sample report, some accounts are past due and others are being paid as agreed. Below this, there is additional information regarding the status of the account in previous months.

Next comes a section on accounts with no adverse information. The basic information provided for these accounts is the same as for the accounts in the previous section.

Inquiries

Inquiries come next in the TransUnion credit report. The information is divided into three sections. The first section lists companies who requested a copy of your credit report, the reason for the request, and the date of the request. The next section lists the names of companies who made inquiries because they wanted to make a firm offer of credit or insurance to the consumer and the date that each inquiry was made. The last section indicates the creditors who obtained information from the credit record as part of an account review—maybe to determine whether the terms of the account should be changed—or for some other business transaction related to the consumer.

Consumer Statement and Special Messages

This section of the sample TransUnion report includes a written statement by the consumer and a special message from Trans-Union regarding the frequency with which the consumer's Social Security number has been used over the past 30 days. Your Trans-Union credit report may include a written statement. Also, it may include a different special message or no statement message at all.

Contact Information

The very last part of the TransUnion credit report provides the address and phone number to contact if you have questions about your report or want to initiate an investigation. Although the sample report does not show it, your TransUnion credit report will also probably include a Web site address for initiating an investigation online.

4

Resolving Credit Record Problems through Investigations, Lawsuits, and More

Ten years ago, when Robert and Sylvia were newlyweds, they began receiving a lot of offers for credit cards and quickly succumbed to the allure of buying on credit. They wanted so many things, and using credit cards was an easy way to get them. About a year and a half into their marriage, however, Robert's employer announced that everyone in the company would have to take a pay cut. Soon Robert and Sylvia were in serious financial trouble. With too much debt and too little income, they began to fall behind on their financial obligations.

Eventually, with the help of Consumer Credit Counseling Services (CCCS), a nonprofit debt counseling organization with local chapters around the country, Robert and Sylvia got their finances on track and paid off their debts. However, they were both left with seriously damaged credit histories. Subsequently, they wanted to rebuild their credit so that they could buy a home. As part of the rebuilding process, they had ordered copies of their credit reports from each of the three national credit bureaus. They wanted to make sure that their reports were accurate and to correct any errors they might contain. Robert found some errors in one of his credit records, but although he followed the process for getting them corrected, he began to get frustrated. Every time he thought an inaccuracy had been corrected, it was there the next time he reviewed his credit record.

Robert and Sylvia are not unusual—many consumers ruin their credit histories by taking on more debt than they can handle, and many others, like Robert, have trouble getting errors in their credit records corrected. They learn that it can take a lot of patience and perseverance to get misinformation permanently removed from their credit files. Therefore, this chapter explains all of your options for getting credit record errors corrected, including initiating a credit bureau investigation and filing a lawsuit. The lawsuit information applies to any FCRA-related problem you may have with a credit bureau, information provider, or a user of your credit record information, not just to problems getting misinformation corrected or deleted from your credit record.

This chapter also explains how to deal with negative but accurate information in your credit record and how to file a formal complaint with the FTC or with your state attorney general's office. It further provides basic information about how to get negative tax-related information out of your credit file sooner rather than later by negotiating with a taxing authority.

Credit Record Problems

There is no firm number regarding the percentage of credit records that contain inaccurate information, but some estimates indicate that as many as 90 percent of all credit records do. That consumer credit records contain a lot of errors should not be surprising, given that the credit reporting industry collects more than 2 billion pieces of credit-related information each month and generates hundreds of millions of credit reports annually. That's a lot of information to collect and process, so mistakes are bound to happen. However, it's not just credit bureaus who cause credit record errors. You may, too, if you provide inaccurate information on an application for credit. Your creditors may as well. For example, they may make mistakes when they input information about you into their database or they may provide inaccurate information to a credit bureau.

To help address the credit file accuracy problem, FACTA requires that the FTC, federal banking agencies, and the National Credit Union Administration establish and enforce new guidelines intended to improve the accuracy of the information that creditors and other information providers supply to credit reporting agencies. However, if an information provider violates the new guidelines and the regulations that enforce them, FACTA gives consumers no legal recourse. Also, all but a handful of states are prohibited from passing their own laws to regulate the conduct of information providers. In other words, your only real recourse if you believe that your legal rights under this particular provision of the law have been violated is to complain to the FTC, one of the federal banking agencies, or the National Credit Union Administration, depending on exactly what kind of business you believe violated your rights. The new guidelines were not available at the time this book was written, but the author will provide a summary of them at his Web site <www.johnventura .com> when they are available.

Given the rate of inaccuracy in consumers' credit records, it is important that you carefully review all three of your credit records, once every six months, for any problems. You should also review them prior to applying for new credit that you really need, important insurance, a new job, and so on. When you do, be on the alert for the following kinds of errors, because they tend to be the most common.

- Information about someone else with a name similar to yours is in your credit file.

- Your account information is inaccurate or incomplete. For example, information related to one of your national bank cards might show that the account was delinquent for several months a year ago. However, it does not indicate that you got caught up and have been paying the account on time for the past nine months. Also, in the public records section of your report, there might be no indication that the tax lien the IRS put on your home for unpaid taxes has been removed.
- There is outdated information in your credit report. In most cases, negative information can only be reported for seven years, although bankruptcies and some other kinds of information can be reported longer.
- Information about the accounts your former spouse opened in his or her own name appears in your credit file.
- Your name is misspelled, your address is wrong, or your Social Security number is incorrect.

If you discover problems in your credit record, correct them as soon as possible. Also, if you find a problem in one report, it's a good idea to order your reports from the other two major credit bureaus to find out if they contain the same error. Because the three national credit bureaus sometimes share information with one another, it's possible that they may share misinformation about you.

FACTA Helps Consumers Monitor the Information in Their Credit Records

With the passage of FACTA, monitoring the information in your credit records has gotten somewhat easier. Prior to FACTA, the only way to know when negative information had been added to one of your credit files was to review each of them on a regular basis. Although reviewing your credit files is still essential, FACTA now says that whenever a financial institution such as a bank, savings and loan, or credit union that you have an account with that provides credit bureau with negative information about

> ## WARNING
>
> FACTA includes a loophole that makes a financial institution not legally liable if it fails to provide a consumer with the appropriate notice, assuming that at the time of the failure it had "reasonable policies and procedures" in place to comply with the law, or if it believed that is was legally prohibited from contacting the consumer.

your account, and assuming it furnishes that information in the normal course of its business, it must notify you in writing about the negative information it has furnished within 30 days of doing so. The notice may come with your account statement, with a notice telling you that you have defaulted on an account, or with any correspondence the financial institution may send you. Regardless of how you receive the information, FACTA requires that the notification be "clear and conspicuous." Interestingly, the law also allows financial institutions to send you a notice about negative information without actually reporting that information to credit bureaus. Also, once a financial institution has sent you an initial notice about any negative account information it may have furnished to a credit bureau, it is not obligated to provide you with notices about additional negative information it may report to the credit bureau about the same account, transaction, extension of credit, or consumer in the future.

Correcting Problems in Your Credit Record

You have two basic options for getting inaccurate credit record information corrected or deleted. You can contact the credit reporting agency reporting the information, or contact

the provider of the information. If you contact the credit bureau
you can:

- Complete the investigation request form that will probably come with your credit report if you order it through
  the mail or by phone.
- Dispute the information online at the Web site of the
  credit bureau. You can file an online dispute at:

  Equifax   <www.econsumer.equifax.com/
                 consumer/forward.ehtml?forward=
                 investigation>
  Experian   <www.experian.com/yourcredit>
  TransUnion   <www.transunion.com/investigate>

- Call the credit bureau. Your credit report or the investigation form should provide a phone number to call. If it
  does not, Chapter 2 provided toll-free numbers for each
  of the three credit bureaus.

Initiating an investigation with an information provider is
discussed later in this chapter.

If you decide to mail in your investigation form and you need
more room than the form provides to explain the problem, use
another sheet of paper and then staple it to the form. Also, if you
have any documentation that helps prove that the information
is incorrect, make copies and attach them to the form as well.

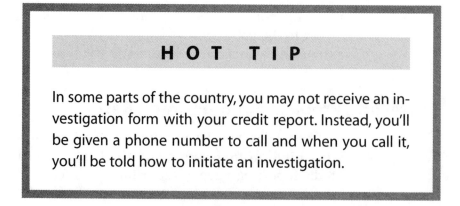

HOT TIP

In some parts of the country, you may not receive an investigation form with your credit report. Instead, you'll
be given a phone number to call and when you call it,
you'll be told how to initiate an investigation.

Your documentation might include copies of canceled checks, receipts, account statements, correspondence between you and an information provider, the document showing that the IRS released the lien it had placed on your property, and so on.

Once you have filled out the investigation request form, make a copy of the form and send it along with copies of all of your backup materials to the credit bureau. File everything away for safekeeping. You may need the information later if you have to sue the credit bureau (or the information provider) over the information you want corrected. Send your request by certified mail and ask for a return receipt. When you get the signed receipt back, file it with the rest of your information related to the problem in your credit report.

If you prefer to initiate your investigation online, be aware that although the process is quick and easy, you have no means of submitting backup information, which may be a problem if you file a lawsuit to get your credit record corrected. Also, some online investigation forms require that you explain your problem by making it fit into one of the problem categories listed on the form. None of those categories may accurately describe your particular problem. Also, the form may provide you with little space to write additional information related to the error you want investigated. Once you have completed the online form, be sure to print a copy and file it away.

HOT TIP

If you dispute information in your credit report online, be sure to print a copy of the completed dispute form. You will need this written record if you decide to sue over the information later.

After you've initiated an investigation, the credit bureau must respond to you within 30 days of receiving your request. If you don't hear from the credit bureau within this period, contact it to learn the status of the investigation.

Frivolous or Irrelevant Investigations

A credit bureau can refuse to conduct an investigation if it has reason to believe that your request is frivolous or irrelevant. However, it must inform you in writing of its decision not to investigate and tell you why it believes that your request is frivolous or irrelevant. It must also tell you in writing what other information it would need from you before an investigation could move forward.

FCRA Requirements for Investigations

The FCRA requires that credit bureaus conduct a "reasonable reinvestigation" of a credit record problem after a consumer initiates an investigation through a credit bureau. The law also establishes a time line for the investigation. For example, it gives credit bureaus and information providers 30 days to investigate a possible credit record problem, promptly correct the problem if they confirm that one exists, and inform you in writing of the outcome of their investigation. However, if you provide them with additional documentation during that 30-day investigation period, the investigation can go on for another 15 days. Once the investigation is over, the credit bureau must send you a written notice of its findings within five days.

The credit bureau must contact the provider of the information you are disputing within five business days of receiving your request for an investigation so that the information provider can certify to the credit bureau whether or not the information is correct. If you have provided the credit bureau with documentation that helps prove the problem, the credit bureau must share it with the information provider.

> # WARNING
>
> If information in your credit record is corrected or deleted after an investigation and then later the credit bureau receives proof that the information you disputed was correct, it can put the information back into your credit file.

If the investigation confirms that you are correct—there *is* an error in your credit record—the information must either be corrected or removed from your credit file. The credit bureau must also promptly notify the provider of the information about the action it took. In turn, the provider must correct or delete the information in its own database, depending on whether the information is inaccurate or wrong. If the information is partially correct, the provider must block it. However, if the information providers conducts its own investigation and concludes that the information you disputed is totally accurate, not just partially accurate, despite the conclusion of the credit bureau, it can continue reporting it to credit bureaus. If the credit bureau cannot confirm whether the information is accurate within the 30-day investigation period, the information must be removed from your credit record.

Problems with Credit Bureau Investigations

Although use of the word *investigation* implies that credit bureaus and information providers will thoroughly research whether there is a problem in your credit record, the word is really a misnomer. Most investigations are not thorough. Therefore, errors do not always get corrected on a timely basis. In fact, some consumers spend years trying to resolve problems in their credit records. Many others give up eventually and pay the price in terms of lost opportunities, a higher cost of credit, and so on.

Here are some of the key problems with credit bureau investigations:

- They are often conducted by low-paid, overworked employees who are neither trained nor motivated to get at the truth or to truly assist consumers. Furthermore, they must understand the nature of a consumer's problem and then correctly categorize the problem on a standard form or prepare a written explanation of the problem. If they miscategorize the problem or don't explain it accurately and completely, the form will not tell the information provider exactly why a consumer believes that his or her credit record is inaccurate.

- Some investigation requests are processed by computers, not by human beings. In these cases, there is little opportunity for the details and nuances of a consumer's credit record problem to be thoroughly explained to an information provider.

- When an information provider receives an investigation request form from a credit bureau, it may not make a real effort to determine if the information it provided to the credit bureau is accurate or inaccurate. Instead, it may just check to confirm whether the information the consumer says is wrong matches the information in its database, which may also be incorrect. Therefore, if it made an error, that error won't be discovered.

At the End of a Credit Bureau Investigation

When a credit bureau completes its investigation, it is obligated to notify you in writing about its findings. It must also send you the following:

- A revised copy of your credit report if it was changed in any way as a result of the investigation

- A notice that upon your request the credit bureau will provide you with a description of the process it used during its investigation
- A notice that you can add a written statement to your credit file if you disagree with the outcome of the investigation
- A notice that if the information you disputed was inaccurate or couldn't be verified, you can ask the credit bureau to provide a corrected version of your credit report to any employer who reviewed your old credit record within the past two years or anyone else who reviewed it within the previous six months. (Twelve months for residents of Maryland, New York, and Vermont.) However, you must provide the credit bureau with a list of exactly who you want to receive the report and you may be charged for the reports it sends out. Be sure to ask for written confirmation that the reports were actually sent.

If Your Credit Record Gets Corrected

If after conducting its investigation, a credit bureau corrects an error in your credit record, deletes out of date information or information it was unable to verify, order another copy of your report after a couple of months. That way, you can be sure that the problem has not reappeared because of a computer glitch or a human error.

If the misinformation in the credit file that one credit bureau is maintaining on you gets corrected, it may automatically get corrected in the credit files of the other credit bureaus if those files contain the same error. This is because the Consumer Data Industry Association (CDIA) maintains an automated system—the Automated Consumer Dispute Verification system—to facilitate the sharing of credit record corrections among the three national credit bureaus. However, this system only works if the information provider involved in an investigation participates in the system. Participation is voluntary, but increasing. Therefore, to make sure that an error that appeared in more than one of your credit files has been corrected, order a copy of your credit record from the other credit bureaus. If they are still reporting the inaccuracy, contact the information provider that participated in the investigation and ask it to notify them about the correction. If this does not resolve your problem, you will have to initiate separate investigations with each of the other credit bureaus.

If Errors Reappear in Your Credit Report

Many consumers discover that credit record information that they thought had been corrected or deleted reappears in their credit records. Sometimes this happens because the credit bureau subsequently receives proof that the information was accurate, but other times it is because of a credit bureau error.

To help prevent inaccurate information from being reinserted into a consumer's credit record, the FCRA says that credit reporting agencies must maintain "reasonable procedures designed to prevent the reappearance of deleted information." However, since the law does not define "reasonable procedures," the impact of this provision is questionable. Also, before information that was changed or deleted can be reinserted into a credit file, the provider must certify in writing to the credit bureau that the information is complete and accurate. In addition, within five business days of the reinsertion, the credit bureau must notify the consumer in writing of its action. It must also give the consumer the name, address, and phone number, if "reasonably available," of the information provider and tell the consumer about the right to have a written statement added to his or her credit record explaining why the consumer believes that it is inaccurate. Written statements are discussed later in this chapter.

When a Credit Bureau Investigation Does Not Correct a Problem in Your Credit Record

If the investigation you initiate does not correct the error in your credit record, you can:

- Locate new or additional information that helps prove the error in your credit record. Make copies of the information and mail them with a cover letter to the information provider. Send the letter certified mail, return receipt requested. Be sure to make a copy of your letter for your records. In your cover letter, ask the information provider to correct your credit record and to send a notice of the correction to all of the credit bureaus it reports to and to you as well. See Figure 4.1 for a sample letter. Also, ask to be sent a copy of the letter(s) that it sends to each credit bureau.
- Prepare a written statement explaining why you believe that the information in your credit file is wrong and send it to the credit bureau. Your statement will become a part of your credit record. The next section of this chapter discusses written statements.
- Meet with a consumer law attorney who has specific experience representing consumers who are having problems with credit bureaus and information providers. A letter from the attorney may get you the result you want, or you may have to file a lawsuit. Hiring an attorney and filing a lawsuit are discussed later in this chapter.
- File a complaint against the credit bureau and/or information provider with the FTC. If your state has a credit reporting law, you should also file a complaint with your state attorney general's office.
- Contact the organizations listed in Figure 4.2.

Written Statements

The FCRA gives you the right to prepare a written statement of up to 100 words that explains why you believe that your credit record is in error. (The statement can also explain negative but accurate information in your credit record.) The credit bureau must make the statement a part of your credit file so that it will be available to anyone who reviews it. You should know however that the value of a written statement is becom-

FIGURE 4.1
Letter to an Information Provider Regarding an Error in Your Credit Report

(Date)

(Name and Address of Creditor)

Dear Sir or Madam: (Direct your letter to the credit manager.)

Recently, I requested a copy of my credit report from (name of credit bureau). In reviewing the report, I discovered a problem(s) relating to the account I have with you. My account number is _____. (Provide account number.)

The problem(s) is: (Describe the problem(s) as clearly and succinctly as possible.). I have enclosed documentation that supports the fact that the information related to this account is inaccurate. Therefore, I would appreciate you checking your records and advising me of your findings. If you determine that the information you have been reporting is inaccurate, please provide the correct information to all of the credit bureaus you work with and direct them to make the appropriate change(s) in my credit files.

In addition, please send me a copy of whatever you send the credit bureaus in response to this letter. Please send it to me at (your complete mailing address).

If you need to reach me by phone, call (area code/telephone number).

Thank you for your prompt attention to this request.

Sincerely,

(Signature)

ing more and more limited. This is because computers are reviewing a growing number of credit applications, which means that your statement may not be seen or read by a human being. Also, a growing number of decision makers are using credit scores to make decisions about consumers, rather than reviewing the

FIGURE 4.2
Helpful Organizations

Here are some nonprofit organizations that may be able to help you resolve a problem with a credit bureau and/or an information provider.

- *National Association of Consumer Advocates (NACA).* NACA is a nonprofit organization of consumer law attorneys and other consumer advocates that helps consumers deal with unfair or abusive business practices, including credit bureaus and creditors who abuse the FCRA. NACA can provide you with a referral to a consumer law attorney in your area who is a NACA member. To get a referral, call 202-452-1989 or go to the NACA Web site at <www.naca.net>.

- *National Consumer Law Center (NCLC).* NCLC is a nonprofit organization that helps advocates for low-income consumers deal with a variety of financial and legal problems. The NCLC also refers consumers to consumer law attorneys in their area who can assist them. To reach the NCLC, call 617-542-8010 or go to <www.consumerlaw.org>.

- *National Foundation for Consumer Credit (NFCC).* This nonprofit organization has a network of credit/debt counseling offices around the country, including the offices of Consumer Credit Counseling Services. To locate the NFCC office nearest you, call 800-388-2227 or go to the NFCC Web site, <www.nfcc.org>.

- *Public Interest Research Group (PRIG).* This is a national, nonprofit organization that works on behalf of consumers. Among other things, it produces reports and fact sheets on credit bureaus and credit reports as well as on identity theft. You can learn more about it at <www.pirg.com>, or you can call the organization at 202-546-9707.

information in their credit records. For these reasons, it is a good idea whenever you apply for credit, insurance, and the like, and you know that your credit record or credit score will be considered during the decision making process, to provide the appropriate decision maker with a copy of your written statement.

HOT TIP

If you need help preparing a written statement, the FCRA requires that credit reporting agencies have personnel available to assist you.

Another Option for Resolving Problems in Your Credit Record

FACTA now gives consumers an explicit right under certain circumstances to initiate an investigation of a problem in their credit record directly with the provider of that information, rather than with the credit bureau that is reporting the information. This right does not apply if a credit repair organization initiates the investigation on a consumer's behalf. The circumstances under which this right applies will be defined in regulations to be developed by the FTC, the federal banking agencies, and the National Credit Union Administration, and will be explained at the author's Web site <www.johnventura.com> once the regulations are issued.

To initiate an investigation directly with the provider of the information you dispute, you must submit your dispute notice to the provider at the address it specifies for such disputes. Your notice must identify the information you are disputing and explain the basis for your dispute. Also, you must furnish the provider with any substantiating information in may request. In turn, the information provider must investigate the information you dispute, including reviewing all of the information you have submitted, and it must complete its investigation within 30 days of receiving your request (within 45 days if you give the providers additional information relevant to the dispute within the 30-day investigation period). If the provider concludes that the disputed information is inaccurate, it must promptly notify each of the credit bureaus to which it reported the information and supply them with the correct information.

An information provider is not required to conduct an investigation if you do not provide it with the information it needs to do so, if it decides your request is "frivolous or irrelevant," or if it decides that your dispute is "substantially the same" as one that you may already have initiated with the credit reporting agency. Under these circumstances, the creditor must inform you of its refusal to investigate that fact by mail, or by any other means of communication that you may have authorized, within five business of receiving your request. The provider must also explain why it considers your request to be "frivolous or irrelevant," and what additional information you would need to sup-

HOT TIP

Initiating an investigation with an information provider rather than with a credit bureau may be a better option because it is more likely that you can solve your problem by talking to a human being, which may make resolving your problem easier to accomplish. Also, presently there is nothing in the law that says a credit bureau can refuse to conduct an investigation into a problem in your credit file after the information provider investigated the same information and your credit file was not corrected as a result. Although this discrepancy may change eventually, until it does, if your efforts to correct a problem in your credit file directly with the information provider don't work out, contact the credit bureau next.

ply in order for and investigation to move forward. However, because this information may be general and not specific to your particular problem, it may not help you.

Formal Complaints

If you cannot get your credit record corrected, it's a good idea to file a formal complaint with the FTC. You can explain your problem, the efforts you have made to resolve it, and the outcome of those efforts.

There are several ways to file a complaint with the FTC:

- Call the FTC at 877-382-4357 or 202-326-2222.
- File a complaint online at <www.ftc.gov>.
- Mail a complaint letter to Federal Trade Commission, Credit Practices Division, Washington, DC 20580 or send it to the FTC office responsible for your region of the country (addresses of the FTC's regional offices are listed in the Appendix). For a sample letter, see Figure 4.3.

After receiving your complaint, don't expect the FTC to take any action against the credit bureau or information provider on your behalf alone. However, if it receives a sufficient number of complaints about that particular business or specific industry

---

HOT TIP

You can file a complaint with the FTC regarding any kind of problem you may have with a credit bureau, an information provider, or a user of your credit record information. The complaint process does not apply just to investigations.

FIGURE 4.3
Letter to the Federal Trade Commission

(Date)

Federal Trade Commission
Bureau of Credit Practices
Washington, DC 20580

Dear Sir or Madam:

    I am writing to register a complaint about (name of company), located at (address of company). A description of my problem with this company follows.

    (Succinctly describe the problem you have been trying to resolve and how the problem has affected your ability to get credit, employment, insurance, or other. Include a chronology of events that illustrates how long you have been working to resolve the problem, the various steps you have taken, and people you have spoken with. Detail the response of company representatives, and when possible, include the names and titles of the persons you have spoken with.)

    While I understand that you do not take action on behalf of individual consumers, I want you to be aware of the troubles I have been experiencing with (name of company). I hope that if you receive enough complaints, you will do what you can to make sure that this company cannot harm other consumers as it has harmed me.

Sincerely,

(Your Signature)

---

practice, it may file a class action lawsuit about the credit reporting agency or information provider, or it may ask Congress to address the problem by amending the FCRA. Also, as a result of the FACTA amendments, when you complain about a credit reporting agency, the FTC is now obligated to pass along your complaint to that agency. In turn, the credit bureau must make

> ## HOT TIP
>
> If you mail the FTC a complaint letter, attach copies of any correspondence and other documentation that will help illustrate your problem and the efforts you have made to resolve it.

certain that it met all its legally mandated obligations when it handled your complaint, and must report its findings to the FTC, together with any actions it may take as a result of its review. In addition, the credit bureau must maintain records documenting how it dealt with your complaint for a specific time period.

Lawsuits

The FCRA gives you the right to sue a credit reporting agency and/or an information provider if you cannot get a problem in your credit record corrected. You may also be able to file a lawsuit against a credit bureau, a user of credit record information, or a provider of information, if it violates your FCRA rights

> ## WARNING
>
> With the passage of FACTA, your right to sue has been limited in many instances, in response to pressure from the credit reporting agencies and financial industries.

in some other way. Figure 4.4 highlights some of the problems you are entitled to sue for according to the FCRA.

You can sue for actual and punitive damages. Actual damages, which can be financial or intangible, compensate you for

---

FIGURE 4.4
Examples of the Kinds of Lawsuits You Can Bring under the FCRA

Lawsuits against a Credit Bureau

- *The information in your credit record is inaccurate.* You cannot sue just because of an inaccuracy. You must be able to prove that you were harmed by the inaccuracy and that the credit reporting agency did not follow "reasonable procedures" to keep your credit record information as accurate as possible. Or you must prove that the procedures existed but were not consistently followed and that there is no reason to think that inconsistent use of the procedures will continue in the future.

- *Your credit report contains outdated information.*

- *Your identity was stolen.* You must have been unable to get the information related to the identity theft removed from your credit record, even though the credit bureau is aware of the theft.

- *Your credit report was furnished to someone else for a purpose that is not allowed by the FCRA.*

- *You were not given the chance to opt out of prescreening.*

- *A credit bureau did not disclose the information in your credit file to you.*

- *Your dispute was not handled properly.*

- *Previously deleted information was reinserted into your credit record.*

(continued)

FIGURE 4.4
Examples of the Kinds of Lawsuits You Can Bring, continued

Lawsuits against a Provider of Credit Record Information

- *The information provider mishandled your dispute.*

- *The information provider gave incomplete information about you to a credit bureau.*

- *The information provider provided false or misleading information about you to a credit bureau.*

- *Your identity was stolen.* You must have been unable to get information for an account that the identity thief opened in your name removed from your credit record, even though the creditor knows about the theft.

Lawsuits against a User of Credit Record Information

- *A business or individual obtained or used your credit record information without a legally permissible purpose or under false pretenses.*

- *An information user failed to provide you with required notices related to the use of your credit record information.* These notices include adverse action notices based on your credit record information. They also include notices that, under certain circumstances, you are supposed to receive before credit record information can be reviewed, for example by employers and government agencies that are trying to collect past due child support.

the harm that a credit bureau and/or information provider did to you. Intangible damage may include: emotional distress, anxiety, depression, humiliation or embarrassment, damage to your reputation, and loss of privacy. Punitive damages are awarded to punish a defendant for a particular behavior and to help deter the defendant from repeating the behavior again.

WARNING

Winning a credit record-related lawsuit can be tough to do, so don't act as your own attorney. You need the help of a consumer law attorney who has experience handling such lawsuits. Not all consumer law attorneys do.

If the court finds the defendant in your lawsuit negligent in not complying with the FCRA, you will be entitled to collect statutory damages ranging from $100 to $1,000, depending on the court's decision, as well as court costs and attorney fees. If the court decides that the defendant willfully violated your FCRA rights, you can also collect punitive damages plus court costs and attorney fees.

If someone obtains a copy of your credit record under false pretenses or for a reason that is not permissible under the FCRA, you can sue for actual damages or $1,000, whichever is greater. The court may also award you punitive damages plus attorney fees and court costs if you win the lawsuit.

Figure 4.5 provides you with some examples of damage awards in some recent FCRA-related lawsuits.

If you have a strong case, a consumer law attorney will probably represent you on a contingency basis. This means that the attorney will get paid by taking a percentage of any money you may win in your lawsuit. If you lose, you won't owe the attorney a fee, although your agreement with the attorney will probably require that you reimburse him or her for your lawsuit-related expenses.

FIGURE 4.5
Damage Awards in Recent FCRA-Related Lawsuits

Here are examples of the kinds of awards that courts have made recently in FCRA-related lawsuits.

- $4,000 in compensatory damages and $42,500 in punitive damages to a consumer who had trouble getting a credit record corrected

- $10,000 to a consumer in compensation for the stress, anxiety, humiliation, and injury to his reputation, his family, and his sense of well-being stemming from a credit record problem

- $125,000 in punitive damages plus attorney fees and court costs totaling $54,692 from two defendants who had obtained a consumer's credit report under false pretenses

- An award of $30,000 to compensate a consumer for the mental anguish and embarrassment caused by an incorrect credit file plus $20,700 in attorney fees

- An award of $15,000 in compensatory damages and $25,000 in punitive damages because a consumer's report did not show that certain debts had been satisfied and the consumer could not get the report corrected

- $75,000 to a consumer because a bank had willfully reported false information about that consumer to credit reporting agencies

How to Find a Good Consumer Law Attorney

The best way to find a qualified consumer law attorney is to contact the National Association of Consumer Advocates (NACA) and/or the National Consumer Law Center (NCLC). Both organizations are profiled in Figure 4.2, Helpful Organizations.

Once you have some attorney names, call them to find out if they offer a initial free consultation session and schedule a meeting with those that do. At the start of your meetings, ask each attorney the following questions:

- How long have you been practicing consumer law, and what percentage of your practice do lawsuits related to credit record problems represent?
- How strong a case do you think I have?
- What are your recommendations regarding the best way to resolve my credit record problem?
- Will you take my case on a contingency basis? If yes, will I have to pay your expenses if I lose, and can you give me an estimate of what they will amount to? If the attorney won't represent you on a contingency basis, find out how the attorney will charge for his or her services and the attorney's hourly rate.
- What information will you need from me if I hire you?

Once you have decided on an attorney, be sure to get a signed contract or letter of agreement before you pay any money. The contract or letter should spell out the services the attorney will provide and how much they will cost and specify the duration of your relationship.

What an Attorney Will Consider before Agreeing to Take Your Case

The attorneys you meet with will consider a variety of factors to determine if you have a winnable case. Assuming you do have a good case, the attorney you hire will take many of these same factors into consideration when deciding how best to build your case, whether it should be brought in state or federal court, and so on. Those factors include the following:

- *The facts of your case.* The more the facts point to a clear injustice, the better your chances of winning your lawsuit.
- *Whether you suffered a direct injury as a result of the FCRA violation.* Examples of direct injury include being denied credit or turned down for a job because of misinformation in your credit report. You must prove that you

asked the credit bureau to correct the misinformation but that it was not corrected.

• *The quality of the information available to the attorney to help build your case.* If there is not enough good information to build a strong case, you may not be able to win your lawsuit, even if you have been harmed by a credit bureau, information provider, or information user. Later in this chapter, I discuss things you can do to help build a case.

• *How you have been harmed.*

• *Whether or not the harm done to you was the result of an innocent, unintentional error.* You won't have a case if it was.

• *Whether the attorney can or should use the FCRA or your state's credit reporting law to bring your lawsuit.*

• *Exactly whom should be sued.* Depending on the facts of your case, your lawyer may want to sue the credit bureau, an information provider, the user of the information, or a combination of parties.

• *Who can be called as witnesses on your behalf.*

• *How much the attorney could sue for.*

• *Whether the attorney could use other laws as the basis of a lawsuit.* You may be able to use other laws if there are problems using the FCRA or your state credit reporting law or if you would prefer not to incur the time and expense of a federal lawsuit.

How You Can Help Build Your FCRA Case

One of the keys to protecting your FCRA rights is good record keeping. When you are choosing an attorney, your records will help the attorneys you meet with decide if you have a good case against a credit bureau, information provider, or a credit record information user. Also, once you hire an attorney, your records will help him or her understand the facts of your case, build your lawsuit, and determine how much to ask for in damages.

Here are examples of the information you should keep.

- *A record of the date(s) that you request a copy of your credit record.* If you put your request in writing, keep a copy of the letter.
- *A record of the date that you request that a credit bureau investigate information in your credit record.* You should also keep a copy of your completed investigation request form.
- *Copies of all letters and written notices you receive or send related to a credit record problem.* This information might include, among other things, notices that you were denied a job or promotion because of information in your credit record or that your rental housing application was rejected for the same reason.
- *Receipts, phone bills, check registers, and other records that document any expenses you incurred related to your dealings with a credit bureau, information provider, or information user.*
- *Copies of any e-mails you may receive from a credit bureau, information provider, or information user related to a problem you are trying to resolve.*
- *Records of any unpaid time you missed from work to resolve a credit record problem.* Note the date that you took the time off, how long you took off, the exact purpose of the time off, and how much it cost you in lost wages and out-of-pocket expenses.
- *Copies of doctor bills and medication receipts,* if you have experienced depression, lack of sleep, or something similar, as a result of your credit record problems and had to get professional help.
- *Written and dated descriptions of any conversations you had with the representative of a credit bureau, information provider, or information user regarding your problem.* Be sure to note the details of any promises that may have been made to you as well as the name of the person you spoke with and the person's title. Write down

your notes as soon as you can after you finish your conversation, when the details of the conversation are fresh in your mind.

- *Notes describing any embarrassment, humiliation, or loss of reputation you may have experienced.* Your suffering may be due to inaccurate information in your credit record or because someone who was not entitled to review your credit record used the information to steal your identity or sold the information to others, etc.

You should collect and file these kinds of information as a matter of course whenever you are dealing with a credit bureau, information provider, and the like, just in case there is a problem later. Your record-keeping system does not need to be sophisticated or elaborate. Some file folders will do.

Lawsuits You Can Bring under the FCRA

Not being able to get information corrected in your credit file is just one example of the kinds of problems that might support your filing an FCRA-related lawsuit against a credit bureau, information provider, or user of information in your credit record. Figure 4.4 shows some of the most common reasons for these lawsuits.

Negative but Accurate Account Information

According to the FCRA, most negative information can remain in your credit file and be reported for up to seven years. However, some negative information can remain longer, including the following:

- A bankruptcy can be reported for up to ten years after the date that it was filed. However, all members of the CDIA, including the three national credit bureaus, report a Chapter 13 bankruptcy for just seven years, assuming the bankruptcy was successfully completed.

WARNING

Under pressure from the credit reporting and credit card industries, when Congress passed FACTA it decided to prohibit individual states from passing or enforcing their own laws related to some of the most problematic aspects of credit reporting and financial privacy, and from enforcing certain aspects of existing laws related to credit reporting and financial privacy. This decision represents a significant loss for consumers who may be harmed by a credit bureau, an information provider, or a user of credit record information, because it is easier and less expensive to bring a lawsuit in state court than in federal court, and because the penalties for violating state law are often more substantial that those that apply when a consumer uses federal credit reporting law to sue. Many of FACTA's prohibitions and pre-emptions vis a vis state laws also apply to identity theft problems, which are discussed in Chapter 10.

- Unpaid tax liens can be reported until they are paid.
- Judgment liens (liens that are not the result of unpaid taxes but of some other type of legal problem) can be reported until the lien is satisfied or the applicable statute of limitation expires.

If negative but accurate information is in your credit file, you can prepare a 100-word written statement that explains the reason for the negative information. This can be a good idea if you feel that there is a good explanation for the information and that your explanation could help you get the credit, employment, insurance, or housing you want. For example, you may not have any health insurance, and the medical bills related to your spouse's cancer surgery caused you to file for bankruptcy. Or you may have lost your job unexpectedly and used up all of your savings during the six months that you were out of work. Your written statement should also explain what you have done to get your finances back on track. Chapter 2, in "The Scoop on Credit Scores," explains why such explanations are becoming increasingly useless.

Adding Information to Your Credit Record

As Chapter 2 explained, some of your creditors may not report information about you to each of the three national credit bureaus. Other creditors may only report information under certain circumstances. Therefore, when you review each of your credit files, you may discover that information about accounts with good payment histories is missing. If you feel that the missing information would improve your credit history, you may be able to get it added to your credit file. However, credit bureaus are not obligated to comply with your request in most situations. Even so, it may be worth the effort, depending on what is in your credit record now and the significance of the information you want added.

Examples of information you may want to add to your credit record include the following:

- Past loans with positive payment histories
- Active accounts with good payment histories
- The history of your mortgage loan, assuming your mortgage payments are not being reported
- Settlements on tax liens, judgments, or debts you disputed

One way to add information is to argue that your credit file is incomplete and to ask that the credit reporting agency— whichever one is not reporting the information—correct the

FIGURE 4.6
Letter to Add Information to Your Credit Record

(Date)

(Address)

Dear Sir or Madam:

In reviewing the credit file you maintain on me, I noted that my credit record does not include certain information that I feel is important to a complete portrait of me as a credit-using consumer. Therefore, I request that you add the following account information to my credit file. (Include a copy of your credit report, and specify the account information you would like added to it. Note relevant account numbers, and provide the complete name[s] and address[es] of applicable creditor[s].)

If you need additional information from me, you can reach me at (area code/ telephone number and mailing address).

Please let me know if there will be a fee involved. Thank you for your assistance.

Sincerely,

(Signature)

Full name _____

Identification number (if you are contacting Experian) _____

Social Security number _____

Birth date _____

Spouse's name _____

Current address _____

_____

Previous addresses for the past five years _____

_____

_____

_____

_____

file by adding the missing information. If the credit bureau agrees to comply with your request, it may ask you for written verification that the information you want added is accurate. In turn, you will have to ask the creditor related to the missing information to provide that verification. Also, the credit bureau may charge you a fee for adding the information. If the credit bureau refuses to comply with your request, you can get the information into your credit record by preparing a written statement.

Another option is to contact the creditor that is not reporting the positive information you want in your credit record and ask it to submit the information to all three national credit bureaus, or to whichever ones it is not reporting to. Again, make your request in writing.

If neither of these approaches works, contact a consumer law attorney who has FCRA experience. The attorney may be able to help you get your positive information added because the attorney will be more familiar with all of the ins and outs of the law, and may be able to identify some provision that can be used to get the missing information into your credit file. Another, somewhat less satisfactory option is to prepare a written statement about the missing information and provide it together with a written statement from the creditor verifying the accuracy of the missing information, whenever you apply for new credit, a new job or a promotion, insurance, or a place to rent.

Negotiating with a Taxing Authority

If your credit record has been damaged because you have an outstanding tax debt and a taxing authority has placed a lien on your property, the sooner you can get caught up on your taxes and get the lien removed the better. If you owe money to the IRS or to your state income tax authority and you can't pay your taxes in full in a lump sum, you may be able to negotiate an installment payment plan or settle the debt for less than the full amount that you owe. When you settle for less, it is called an Offer in Compromise. Once you are caught up on your taxes, the taxing authority will remove its lien from your property and should begin reporting to credit bureaus that the lien has been removed.

If you owe back property taxes, the taxing authority will not agree to an Offer in Compromise, but you may be able to wipe out your tax debt through an installment payment plan. Depending on its policy, the taxing authority may agree to remove its lien after you begin making your installment payments, or it may require that you pay a certain amount on your tax debt before it will remove the lien.

To initiate negotiations with a taxing authority, you must contact the appropriate office to explain what you want to do and find out whom to talk with and what paperwork you must fill out. If you owe a lot of money in back taxes or if you feel uncomfortable handling your own negotiations, hire a lawyer or a CPA who has experience negotiating with the IRS or with your state/local taxing authority. These professionals will know whether your negotiations have a good chance of succeeding, the best way to initiate the negotiations, what forms to fill out, and so on.

The IRS

If the IRS has placed a lien on your property, the Internal Revenue Code says that the agency can negotiate a compromise on payment of your tax liability, assuming that the liability is not part of a lawsuit and that one or both of the following criteria are met:

- There must be some doubt that you actually owe the amount of money that the IRS says you owe, and you must prove to the IRS that you are not liable for all or part of the tax debt. Canceled checks, copies of tax forms, correspondence, signed agreements, and so on may help you make your case. If you can prove doubt, the amount by which the IRS will reduce your debt will depend on its assessment of just how much doubt exists.

• The IRS must believe that it may never be able to collect the full amount of your tax debt, including penalties and interest.

To determine how much of your total tax debt you can afford to pay, if anything, the IRS will value all of your assets and assess your current and future earnings potential using a set of standard guidelines. It will also confirm that you are up-to-date on all your other IRS income tax obligations, because if you are not, the agency probably won't be open to a compromise.

5

Rebuilding Your Credit

Sam V. sat in my office telling me about the new book he had bought, *Credit Rebuilding Secrets.* The entire time he was talking, I was thinking about how easy it is for people who are desperate to rebuild their credit after financial troubles to be victimized by quick fix schemes. Although the book Sam had purchased was just 37 pages long, he had paid $49.95 for it! When I skimmed its contents, I noted that it was all about a clever way for consumers to create new credit identities for themselves using a fraudulent rebuilding method called "file segregation."

"So what do you think?" Sam asked.

"First of all, some of the suggestions in this book are illegal," I responded. "Plus, did you notice that the book does not provide the name of its author or any information regarding how to get in touch with the publisher? That makes me very suspicious."

Sam looked at the book as if he were seeing it for the first time. "You're right. I was so intrigued by what the book promised, that I did not notice that."

"Sam," I said, "this book is suggesting that you participate in a fraud. When it comes to rebuilding credit, the best advice I can give you is that there are no quick fixes, despite what your book says. It takes time and effort to rebuild a damaged credit history. There are no quick fixes."

I went on to share with Sam the same philosophy and practical advice about credit rebuilding that I share with you in this chapter.

A Creditwise Philosophy

A lot changes when you damage your credit record. The most noticeable change is that it becomes harder to qualify for credit with reasonable terms. Therefore, until you put some distance between yourself and your credit problems, it is best to live on a cash-only basis as much as possible.

It is not unusual for people who have ruined their credit records, and who are trying to live on what they make rather than resorting to high-interest credit, to reassess their values and priorities in life. They may ask themselves what they really want out of life, how important spending and material possessions truly are to them, and whether those things are so important that they are willing to go into debt again to have them. They may also begin to recognize the value of sacrificing and saving for the things they really need or want rather than pay-

---

WARNING

When your credit record is damaged, the credit you qualify for will come with higher than normal interest rates and other unattractive terms of credit, because creditors will consider you a bad credit risk.

ing for them with credit cards so that they can have them right away.

Reassessing your priorities is an important conversation to have with yourself, if your credit history has been seriously damaged because you mismanaged your finances and took on more debt that you could handle. It's especially important if you are ready to begin rebuilding your credit after serious financial difficulties. Based on my experience counseling people who have gotten into serious financial trouble, they tend to share several characteristics.

- *Their desire to spend and to have material things exceeded their ability to pay for what they wanted out of their incomes.* Therefore, they used credit to get those things rather than saving up for them.
- *They did not distinguish between needs or necessities and their desires.* Nor did they distinguish between what they could save for and buy later and what they had to purchase now using credit. In fact, many of these consumers made the mistake of trying to get as much credit as possible and then used it, regardless of whether or not they could afford to make their debt payments.

As a rule, consumers who can distinguish between their needs and their desires, who carefully limit their use of credit, and who are willing to save to get what they want are less apt to get into financial trouble. Sometimes of course, financial trouble can be the result of problems beyond your control—a devastating illness or serious accident and all of the associated medical bills, an unexpected job loss in a poor economic climate, and so on.

It's dangerous to treat credit as a tool for making all of your dreams come true right away. Instead, use it as a tool for purchasing the goods and services that your family truly needs now but cannot afford to buy with cash. Also, use it to purchase things that it might take you many, many years to save for, such as a home or car.

Credit Is Necessary in Today's World

Although there are good arguments for living without credit, the fact is, it's really not realistic in today's world. For example, without credit, it's hard to rent a car, reserve a hotel room, and purchase airline tickets; and buying a house, financing your child's college education, and paying for other big ticket purchases is virtually impossible unless you earn a lot of money. In most instances it's impossible to purchase online unless you have credit. Therefore, if your credit history is seriously damaged, you will want to obtain a limited amount of new credit at reasonable terms as soon as possible.

A Sound Approach to Credit Rebuilding

When you are ready to begin rebuilding your credit history, avoid doing anything that could get you into trouble again. For example, limit the amount of credit you apply for, and don't have multiple bank cards—just one or two will do. Also, shop for the best deals on credit, don't run up your credit card balances, and avoid getting credit just to have it.

Gaining the trust of creditors is key to credit rebuilding. To earn their trust, you must prove to them over time that your money troubles are behind you, that you are a responsible money manager and know how to use credit wisely, and that you will pay all of your debts on time. Proving these things to creditors will take time.

When to Start Rebuilding

You can start rebuilding your credit once the financial difficulties that contributed to your credit record problems are behind you. However, even before you are ready to start rebuilding, you can prepare for that process. In fact, you should prepare before you apply for new credit of any kind.

- Review your credit record with each of the big three credit bureaus for errors as well as for negative but accurate information that you feel merits an explanation with a written statement.
- Correct errors and add written statements to your record as necessary.
- If you have not begun stashing money away in savings, then start. Save something each month, even if it's only a small amount. Having money in savings is like having a financial safety net. Also, you may need money in your savings account to qualify for a bank loan or a national bank card.
- If you still have some credit accounts, make your payments on time. Also, use the accounts only to purchase things you really need and don't have the cash to pay for.
- Develop solid money management skills. Possible sources of help include your local Consumer Credit Counseling Services office, a college or university in your area, and your county extension service. Also, you can find many good personal finance books at your local library, and there is plenty of good information on the Web.

HOT TIP

If you filed for bankruptcy, you don't have to wait until the bankruptcy is no longer being reported in your credit record to begin the credit rebuilding process. You can start rebuilding six to nine months after your bankruptcy is over.

Rebuild Your Credit Step-by-Step

There are a number of important rules of thumb to keep in mind during the credit rebuilding process.

- *It will take time—as long as two to three years—so don't get impatient.* Your credit history did not get ruined overnight, and you can't rebuild it overnight, either.

- *Don't be fooled into thinking that you can speed up the process with the help of a credit fix-it firm.* As Chapter 6 makes clear, that kind of company can't do anything you can't do for yourself, for free. So, unless you don't feel confident about your credit rebuilding abilities, it's a waste of money to pay for help. Furthermore, many of those firms are rip-offs.

- *Apply for a minimum amount of credit.* One or two national bank cards are all you really need, especially since most local and regional retailers accept them. Plus, if you have a lot of bank cards, you may be tempted to use them. Also, potential new creditors will be less inclined to give you credit if they see from your credit record that you have a lot of open credit accounts.

You may be unable to qualify for a regular national bank card right away. You may have to apply for a secured national bank card first. Then, once you have established a history of respon-

---

WARNING

Don't apply for retail store charge cards. Most of those cards come with relatively high rates of interest, and nearly all retailers accept MasterCard and Visa these days.

sible payments on the secured card, you can apply for one that is unsecured. Secured cards are discussed later in this chapter.

Once you have a national bank card, regardless of whether it is secured or unsecured, your goal should be to pay off the card balance each month. In other words, charge something using your card and then pay off the card balance before you use the card again. If you follow this advice, over time you will prove to creditors that you are a responsible credit manager and a good credit risk.

If you do not have a savings account with a local bank, open one. Building your savings is the first step toward getting a bank loan. Once you have between $500 and $1,000 in your savings account, apply to the bank for a small, secured loan. The funds in your savings account can secure it. If the bank where you have your account won't give you a loan, apply for a cash-secured loan with another bank in your area. After you've paid off your first bank loan, apply for a second small loan that is not cash-secured.

The process I've just described is not the only way to re-build a damaged credit history, but it has worked well for many of my clients. The best process for you will depend on your previous credit history and your present circumstances. Remember, however, that regardless of how you rebuild your credit, your goal is not to get all the credit you can but rather to get the credit you really need at the best possible terms.

Getting a Bank Loan

When you are ready to apply to your bank for a loan, call to schedule an appointment with a consumer loan officer. Explain over the phone that you had money troubles in the past and damaged your credit history but that you would like to discuss the possibility of getting a cash-secured loan as part of the credit rebuilding process.

If the loan officer is not interested in working with you because of your credit history, call another bank in your community. Continue calling banks until you find a loan officer willing at least to meet with you to discuss your credit needs.

Banks and Loan Officers

Banks are highly regulated businesses, and they are expected to safeguard their depositors' funds by minimizing the risks they take lending and investing money. In fact, if a bank makes too many high-risk loans, it may lose its charter and be out of business.

The careers of loan officers are in large part determined by the success of the loans they make. In other words, a loan officer who makes lots of well-performing loans is more apt to have a successful banking career than one who makes many loans that perform poorly. Therefore, it's understandable that with a damaged credit history, you are not going to be as attractive to a loan officer as someone with an unblemished record, because you will be considered a bigger risk. For this reason, it may take you a while to locate a loan officer who is willing to lend you money.

If you can't find a loan officer who is willing to do business with you, recontact the loan officers you called who seemed most sympathetic to you or with whom you had the best rapport and ask each of them what you need to do to get a loan. They may tell you that you should save more money or increase your income, or that you just need to wait until there is more distance between you and your financial problems.

When You Meet with a Loan Officer

Once you find a loan officer who is willing to meet with you, ask to be mailed a loan application so you can complete it before your meeting. When you arrive for your appointment with the loan officer, be prepared to explain the following:

- Any negative information that may be in your credit report
- Why you developed financial problems, and what you have done to make certain that they will not reoccur
- How your life has changed since the problems developed, and why you believe that you are a good candidate for a loan despite the problems in your past

Because loan officers are risk averse, be prepared to convince them that you are a good risk. If your financial problems were the result of poor money management skills, tell the loan officer about what you have done to develop better skills. If they developed because of a situation that was beyond your control—your spouse was laid off, you got divorced, or your child was hospitalized, for example—explain how things in your life have changed. Also, be ready to explain the reasons why you want credit again. For example, you and your spouse want to buy a home for your family, you need to replace your car with one that is more reliable, or your children are approaching college age and you will need to borrow money to help pay for their education.

Should your first meeting go well, the loan officer may schedule a second meeting after having time to review your credit report and/or check your credit score, or the loan officer may review this information online during the meeting. The officer will look at your credit record to make sure that you have been honest and forthcoming about all aspects of your financial history and that you have not been applying for a lot of new credit. If the officer seems reluctant to make you a loan, even a secured loan, ask what you need to do to get the loan you want.

If you are approved for a cash-secured loan, the loan will probably be for an amount close to what you have in your savings account. You may be asked to put the loan proceeds in a certificate of deposit (CD) at the bank. You will probably have

HOT TIP

Dress neatly and conservatively for your meeting. Wear something understated—nothing flashy—and no shorts and T-shirts.

a year or so to complete your payments. Be sure to make each payment on time, because your goal is to prove to the loan officer that you can manage your money responsibly and qualify for a second loan that is not cash secured. It usually takes more than a positive payment history on just a single loan to rebuild a damaged credit record.

Getting a Second Loan

After you have paid off your first loan, order a copy of your credit report from each of the three national credit bureaus. Make sure that they accurately reflect your loan payments.

Next, let the loan officer know that you want to apply for a second loan that is not cash secured. If you made all of the payments on your first loan on time, you should not have a problem getting this next loan. If you do, apply to another bank for an unsecured loan. Once you get the loan, pay it off just like the first one, and after that loan is paid off, check your credit history again with each of the national credit bureaus after it's paid in full.

Shopping for a National Bank Card

Before applying for a national bank card—a Visa or Master-Card card—it pays to spend some time understanding the terminology and features of bank cards. There are a lot of offers to choose from, and your goal should be to get the best deal possible on a card.

The best deal is not simply the bank card with the highest credit limit; in fact, a card's credit limit should be one of your least important considerations. Furthermore, if your first bank card is a secured card, the size of your credit limit will depend on how much money you put up as security. Secured bank cards are discussed in the next section of this chapter.

More important factors to consider when you are shopping for a bank card include its annual percentage rate (APR), interest rate, grace period, and fees. For short definitions of these and other important bank card terms of credit, refer to Figure 5.1.

FIGURE 5.1
National Bank Card Features

When you are evaluating which national bank card to apply for, you should consider each card's terms of credit. Some will be better than others, and the better the terms, the less the credit will cost you. Consider the following terms of credit:

- *Interest rate, or monthly periodic rate.* All bank card issuers charge daily interest on an account's unpaid balance. The interest rate you pay will depend on the issuer's terms of credit and the laws of the state where the card issuer is located. If you do not plan on paying your card balance in full every month, go with the card that offers you the lowest possible rate of interest for which you can qualify.

- *Annual percentage rate (APR).* This is the monthly periodic rate expressed as a yearly rate of interest. For example, if your APR is 19 percent, that means that in a year's time, you will have paid 19 percent on your card balance, which equals a monthly periodic rate of 1.58 percent.

- *Balance calculation method.* Bank card companies will use one of several different methods to calculate the amount of interest to add to your card balance each month. The most consumer-friendly methods include the *adjusted balance method* and the *average daily balance excluding new purchases.* The worst methods for consumers are the *two cycle average daily balance excluding new purchases* and the *two cycle average daily balance including new purchases* methods. Other methods are *previous balance* and *average daily balance including new purchases.*

- *Credit limit.* This is the maximum amount of money you can charge on your bank card at any one time.

- *Grace period.* This is the amount of time you have to pay your bank card balance in full each month before interest or finance charges will be added to the balance. If you don't expect to pay your account balance in full each month, the longer the grace period the better. However, some cards do not offer a grace period, and some charge you interest even if you pay your card balance during the grace period.

- *Fees.* Depending on the card, you may have to pay an annual fee, a late fee, a fee for exceeding your credit limit, a fee if the check you send to pay your bank card bounces, and so on.

Secured Bank Cards

Using a secured bank card responsibly is an excellent way to build creditors' trust in your ability to manage credit responsibly and to help you achieve your goal of getting an unsecured card. If a bank issues you a secured card, you will have to secure or collateralize the purchases you make with that card by opening a savings account at the bank or by purchasing a CD from the bank. Then, if you fall behind on your card payments, the bank can get paid by withdrawing money from your savings account or by cashing in your CD. However, if you make your payments in full and on time each month, the bank won't tap your collateral, and you will be building a new, more positive credit history for yourself. Eventually, you should be able to qualify for a regular bank card.

Here are a couple good resources to use to find the best deal on a secured or unsecured bank card that meets your needs.

- Bankrate.com, <www.bankrate.com>
- CardTrak, PO Box 1700, Frederick, MD 21702, <www. cardtrak.com>

If you receive a bank card offer in the mail, don't take it at face value. Most of the information in the offer is meant to sell you the card; the important details are in the fine print. For exam-

WARNING

Don't apply for a lot of bank cards. Every time you apply for one, it will show up in your credit record as another inquiry. A lot of such inquiries are apt to make reputable creditors less interested in working with you.

ple, the card's low, low interest rate may expire after a couple months and then increase significantly, or it may get bumped way up if you are late just one day with your monthly payment. Therefore, carefully evaluate each offer using the terms of credit information in Figure 5.1. Spend as much time and energy shopping for a bank card as you would spend shopping for a new car, a home, or a major appliance. Selecting a bank card is an important decision!

Once You Have a Secured Bank Card

Once you have a secured national bank card, use it to charge necessities only, not frivolous items that you would normally buy with cash. Put aside the cash amount of your charged purchase so that you'll have the money you need to pay your bill in full when it arrives. After you have been using the secured card for six months, order a copy of your credit report from each of the three national credit bureaus to make certain that your payments are being reported accurately.

Try not to carry a balance on your account from month to month. Before you know it, you will have run up a big balance, and you may not be able to afford the monthly payments. Also, maintaining a balance on your bank card is expensive because of the interest you will be paying.

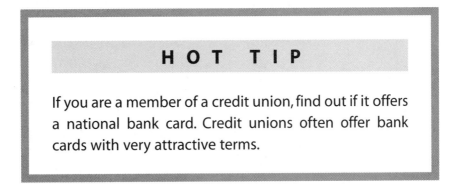

HOT TIP

If you are a member of a credit union, find out if it offers a national bank card. Credit unions often offer bank cards with very attractive terms.

Other Considerations

There are other factors to consider, besides a card's terms of credit, when you are in the market for a secured bank card. For example, you should also consider the following:

- *Application fee.* Is there an application fee, and how much is it? If you pay the fee and then are not approved for the card, can you get it back?
- *Collateral.* How much money or collateral do you have to deposit with the bank for the bank card? The amount will probably range from a few hundred dollars to a few thousand. Do you have the option of putting your deposit collateral in a CD or money market account, where it will earn a slightly higher rate of interest than in a savings account?
- *Rate of interest.* What rate of interest will your deposit earn? The higher the better, obviously.
- *Credit line.* What percent of your deposit will your credit line be? It could range from 50 to 100 percent. The higher the percentage, the better. Also, can you increase your credit limit without increasing your deposit, if you pay your account on time? How soon after you've had use of the card you can increase that limit?
- *Converting.* Can you convert the secured card to an unsecured card? If you can, under what conditions?
- *Tapping the collateral.* If your account becomes past due, when can the card issuer tap your collateral to get payment?

W A R N I N G

The money you use to collateralize a secured bank card will not be available to you.

Also, can you get your collateral back if you close the account, what conditions apply to getting your money back, and will you have to pay a fee if you close the account?

Beware of Bank Card Scams

Some companies deceptively advertise secured and unsecured Visa and MasterCard cards on television, in newspapers, and through the Internet. Usually, their ads try to make you believe that all you have to do to obtain a national bank card is call an 800 or 900 telephone number. The truth is, however, that getting a bank card is almost never that easy. Furthermore, cards that are marketed that way are rarely good deals for anyone other than the company that issues them. Therefore, do not respond to ads like these. If you do, here are some of the problems you may encounter.

- If you call a 900 number, you'll be charged an expensive-fee per minute. The fee will probably range from $.50 to $50 or even more. Most likely, the ad for the bank card will not indicate the cost of your call.
- The ads may not be clear about the terms of the bank card. For example, they may be vague about how much you must deposit as collateral, the size of the application fee (it could be substantial), the amounts of any other fees you will be charged, the APR, and so on.
- After you pay an application fee, you may just receive a list of bank cards for which you can apply; a high interest, high fee card; or nothing at all.

Alternative Ways to Buy on Credit

As this chapter has already explained, rebuilding your credit will not happen overnight. In fact, some of you may not be able to qualify for a conventional bank loan or a national bank card with reasonable terms of credit for many years. Therefore, it pays to be aware of alternative ways to purchase what you need.

Although most of these alternatives will cost more than using conventional credit, if you need a car to get to and from work or if owning a house now is really important to you, the following information may be helpful.

Buying a Home

Most banks will not give you a mortgage loan until your financial problems have been over for at least two to three years and you have completed your bankruptcy. Furthermore, when you do get one, you'll probably have to put down a larger-than-average down payment, and you will probably be charged a higher rate of interest than someone without a negative credit history. With this information in mind, alternative ways to buy a home include the following:

- *Buy a HUD (Department of Housing and Urban Development) home.* These are foreclosed homes originally financed with an insured mortgage from the Federal Housing Administration (FHA), and they tend to be affordable. They can include single-family homes, condominiums, and town houses. Although they are sold as is, you can get some good bargains if you are willing to buy a fixer upper. To find out about the HUD homes for sale in your area, look in your local paper's real estate classified section or call a Realtor in your area.
- *Owner-financed homes.* Some home sellers will finance the purchase of their home to generate a steady stream of income for themselves, perhaps because they are getting ready to retire. These sellers are likely to have less stringent credit requirements than traditional lending institutions. However, they usually require bigger down payments from buyers than a bank, and they may also charge a higher rate of interest.
- *Rent to purchase.* If you've rented a home for a while and the owner likes and trusts you, the owner may be willing to give you a lease agreement with an option to buy.

HOT TIP

A mortgage broker can help you find a loan when your credit is damaged. Mortgage brokers link people who want to borrow money with investors, including mortgage companies. Because of your credit problems, you will probably be considered a high-risk borrower. If you want to work with a mortgage broker, be wary of one who asks for money up front, even if you are promised that you can get your money back if the loan doesn't come through. A reputable broker only gets paid if he or she actually gets you a loan.

Buying a Car

For many people, buying a car is the biggest and most important purchase they will make during their lives. Here are some ways to buy a car even if you have bad credit.

- *Contact your banker.* If you have a good relationship with a banker, schedule an appointment to discuss under what conditions the bank would make you a car loan. The banker will want to know what kind of down payment you can make—the bigger the better—as well as the age of the car you want to buy. A bank may not want to loan you money for a car that is old and not worth a lot. If the bank has to repossess the car, the bank may not be able to get its money back, because the costs of repossessing and selling your car may be greater than what the car will fetch. The banker may want you to have someone cosign your car loan. The cosigner would have to be someone with good credit. By signing your loan agreement with you, your cosigner will be responsible for paying the loan if you can't make the loan payments or just stop making them. Friends and family members are often cosigners, but employers sometimes cosign, too.

- *Look for "bad credit no problem" ads.* In most major cities, some of the larger car dealerships offer high-risk loan programs. Typically, these car dealers will sell you a car no matter what your credit history is, so long as your job is stable, your down payment is big enough, and you don't mind the high interest rate. Pursue this option only if you have no other choice and you absolutely need a new car.

- *Used-car dealers.* Many used-car dealers will finance the purchase of a car if you have a stable job and can make an adequate down payment. However, a loan from a used car dealer won't be a bargain. Also, some used car dealers are shady. For example, they may know nothing about the history of the car you want to buy or whether it's mechanically sound. Most used car dealers sell their cars as is, which means that you could end up buying someone else's problems. Therefore, before you sign any paperwork or pay any money for a used car, have it checked out by a mechanic you know and trust. Don't take the dealer's word that the car runs well and has never been in a wreck.

- *Talk with your friends and relatives.* They may have a car that they don't need anymore and may be willing to sell it to you rather than trading it in or selling it to someone else.

WARNING

If you have a cosigner on a loan and do not make timely payments on it, you will not only damage your credit record but the cosigner's as well.

6

Avoiding Credit Repair Rip-Offs

I first met Carlos S. several years ago. He had come to my office to file for bankruptcy, because he had financed his business with his personal credit cards and then the business had failed. His business troubles, coupled with a divorce, had left Carlos's credit history in a shambles. Now, he was visiting me with his new wife, Michelle.

Michelle had her own financial problems because of her divorce. As part of their divorce settlement, her former husband had agreed to pay off the debts he and Michelle had acquired during their marriage, but he had not followed through on his promises. Unpaid creditors had come after Michelle for their money. Although it meant getting a weekend job, Michelle eventually paid them all. However, when she checked her credit records, she discovered that one of them did not reflect her payments, and showed that she still owed money on an account she had paid off.

Carlos and Michelle were concerned that the misinformation in Michelle's credit record, combined with Carlos's bankruptcy, would prevent them from building the life together that they envisioned. Michelle, especially, was feeling frustrated because she had worked very hard and made many sacrifices to pay off the debts from her former marriage.

During our meeting, Carlos and Michelle told me about an ad they had seen on the Internet for a company that said it could eliminate negative information—even a bankruptcy—from a consumer's credit file. Carlos and Michelle told me they were thinking of working with the company and wanted to know what I thought.

"It sounds like a great deal," Carlos told me.

"It sounds too good to be true," I replied.

I explained that the company ripped off consumers by charging them big bucks to improve their credit records—something they could do themselves for little or no money. I also explained that the FCRA allows credit bureaus to report most negative consumer record information about a consumer for up to ten years, depending on the nature of the information. Therefore, I said, companies that promise to make negative information disappear right away are either lying about what they can do or are going to use illegal methods.

Nearly everyone who has had financial problems wants to have a perfect credit record, and they want it sooner rather than later. However, to achieve that goal, some consumers pay for the assistance of disreputable credit repair firms rather than rebuilding their credit records the legitimate way.

Many reputable debt counseling firms can help consumers correct problems in their credit records and rebuild their credit histories for a reasonable fee. However, many prey on consumers who are uninformed or desperate to get new credit by using quick-fix, illegitimate methods, and they charge consumers a lot of money for their services. In this chapter, I explain how credit fix-it firms work and how they rip off consumers.

What Is a Credit Repair Firm?

Most debt counseling firms are legitimate businesses that work within the law to help consumers resolve problems in their credit records and rebuild their credit. But many others charge exorbitant fees—as much as several thousand dollars—

to make negative credit record information disappear. You've seen their ads: "We can make your bad credit disappear—even bankruptcy," "Bad credit? No problem. Get new credit fast," or, "We can give you a new credit identity—legally," and so on. Some of these firms are little more than mobile con artists who move from place to place to stay one step ahead of the law. They charge unsuspecting consumers a hefty, up-front fee for their services and then skip town, leaving their victims poorer and without the credit record improvements they were promised.

The most important fact you should know about getting help rebuilding your credit record is that a debt counseling or credit repair firm cannot do anything for you that you can't do yourself, for little or no money. For example, the FCRA gives you the right to have inaccurate or outdated information deleted from your credit record and to have written statements added to your credit record. This book describes how to do both. However, the FCRA does not give you the right to get negative but true information removed from your credit record before the date that the law says it can no longer be reported. That same law applies to debt counseling and credit repair firms. As you learned in Chapter 1, the FCRA allows most negative information in your credit record to be reported for seven years, although certain kinds of negative information can be reported for ten years or longer. Therefore, only time can make negative information go away, unless the information is inaccurate. However, if inaccurate information is in your credit record, try to correct that problem by following the advice in Chapter 4, not by hiring a credit repair firm. Figure 6.1 summarizes the steps to take to correct a problem in your credit record.

How to Spot a Disreputable Credit Repair Firm

Some illegitimate credit fix-it firms are easy to spot; others can be more difficult to identify because they market themselves as debt counseling and advice companies or as nonprofit agencies. Here are some signs that a business is a credit repair firm:

FIGURE 6.1
Overview of How to Resolve a Credit Record Problem

1. Ask the credit bureau to investigate the error in your credit record.

2. If the credit bureau corrects your problem, ask it to send a copy of your corrected credit report to any employer who reviewed your credit record within the past two years and to anyone else who reviewed it within the past six months.

3. Wait a few months and then request another copy of your credit report to make sure that the error has not reappeared.

4. If the credit bureau says that the information you are disputing is correct, try to locate new documentation that proves that the information is wrong. You may want to contact the information provider directly and see if you can resolve your problem.

5. If you follow the advice in step #4 and still can't get your credit record corrected, meet with a consumer law attorney who has experience handling FCRA-related problems. It may just take a letter written on your attorney's letterhead to resolve your credit record problem, or you may need to file a lawsuit. If you decide to sue, the lawyer will probably take your case on a contingent fee basis.

6. Write a 100-word statement explaining why you think your credit record is in error. The credit bureau must make the statement a part of your credit file.

7. File a formal complaint with the FTC. If the FTC receives enough complaints about a credit bureau or a credit reporting agency practice, it may take legal action. However, it will not take action on your behalf alone. You should also file a complaint with your state attorney general's office if your state has its own law that applies to credit records.

- The company makes impossibly extravagant promises about what it can do for you, such as, "We can make bankruptcies and other negative information in your credit record disappear."
- The company says it will use "little-known loopholes" in the FCRA to get rid of negative information in your credit record.
- The company claims that despite the negative information in your credit record, it can get you a major bank card.

These bogus firms use a wide variety of techniques to market their services to consumers. For example, they may distribute fliers in parking lots and post them on telephone poles, advertise on television, use direct mail, sell their services through telemarketing, and use the Internet and e-mail to market their services. Credit repair firms that use direct mail or telemarketing to market their services often develop their target marketing lists from court records of people who have filed for bankruptcy.

These firms know that if you are anxious to get rid of negative information in your credit file, you may want to use their services. To help you separate fact from fiction, here are some of the more common claims that disreputable credit repair firms make and the real story behind each claim.

False Claim #1. If you are bankrupt, you won't be able to get credit for ten years.

Fact: Although a bankruptcy will stay in your credit record for up to ten years, creditors have their own standards for granting credit. Many of them will work with bankrupt consumers, especially if the consumers filed for Chapter 13 and their financial problems were due to problems beyond their control—a lost job or unreimbursed medical expenses, for example—and if the consumers have a stable income.

False Claim #2. The company is affiliated with the federal government.

Fact: The federal government does not have a relationship with any of these firms.

False Claim #3. File segregation, a technique used by some credit repair firms to create new, problem-free credit identities for consumers, is legal.

Fact: File segregation, explained later in this chapter, may require you to make false statements on a credit or loan application. If you do, you are committing a federal crime. Also, in some states, file segregation constitutes civil fraud. Furthermore, it is a federal crime to misrepresent your Social Security number and to obtain an employer identification number (EIN) from the IRS under false pretenses, other things some credit repair firms may ask you to do as part of the file segregation process. In addition, if you use the mail or the telephone to apply for credit and provide false information, you could be accused of mail or wire fraud.

Credit Repair Firm Products and Services

In addition to their credit repair services, some credit fix-it firms offer debt consolidation loans, debt counseling services, and national bank cards. (Legitimate debt counseling firms and nonprofit agencies may offer these products and services, too.) However, their loans may come with very high interest rates and substantial up-front fees, and they may insist that you use your home as loan collateral. Even worse, some credit repair firms misrepresent the terms of their loans.

Furthermore, their debt counseling services are often little more than recommendations that you file for bankruptcy, even if taking that step is not your best option. And their national bank card offers may be nothing more than applications for a secured bank card, something you can obtain on your own. Chapter 5 provided you with resources for finding a good bank card.

Credit Repair Techniques

To make problems in your credit record go away, some credit repair firms use techniques that are illegal or, at best, morally questionable. As already noted in this chapter, if you make a false statement on a loan or credit application, misrepresent your Social Security number, or obtain an EIN from the IRS under false pretenses—all things that a credit repair firm may ask you to do—you will be committing a federal crime. Therefore, you must be aware of the techniques credit repair firms commonly use, so that if a firm's marketing come ons don't tip you off to the fact that it is disreputable, its techniques will.

Loopholes

The FCRA gives you the right to challenge any information in your credit record that you don't believe is accurate. As Chapter 4 explained, if a credit bureau can't verify whether the information you are disputing is right or wrong within 30 days of receiving your investigation request, it must immediately delete that information. However, some credit repair firms try to abuse this provision of the law by inundating credit reporting agencies with numerous, repeated requests to delete negative information in a consumer's credit file, regardless of whether the information is accurate or inaccurate. Their goal is to overwhelm the credit bureau with so many requests that it won't be able to respond to all of them within the 30-day deadline.

Another popular credit repair firm technique is to create new, problem-free credit identities for consumers through an illegal technique called file segregation or "skin shedding." Here is how it works. A credit repair firm tells you that for a fee, it can help you get rid of your damaged credit record by establishing a new credit identity for you. If you decide to work with the firm, it will tell you to apply to the IRS for an Employers Identity Number (EIN) and then to use that number rather than your Social Security number whenever you apply for new credit. (An EIN resembles a Social Security number, and it is used by businesses to report information to the IRS and the Social Security Administration.) You will also be instructed to use a new mailing address when you fill out credit applications.

Other credit repair firms advise their clients to send their creditors checks for partial payment on their past-due accounts.

They also advise them to write on those checks that, by cashing it, the creditor (or collection agency) is agreeing to stop its collection efforts and to remove all negative information related to that account from the consumer's credit file. However, many creditors and collection agencies won't accept checks with such conditions, and in some states, they can accept them without honoring the terms of payment written on the checks.

Quick-fix credit repair methods are not only a waste of your hard-earned money but are also morally questionable and sometimes even illegal. Furthermore, if your credit record problems are due to poor money management skills and overuse of credit, you are asking for more financial trouble in the future if you try to speed up the credit rebuilding process by working with a fix-it firm. Your money and time would be better spent if you enrolled in a money management class or if you figured out why your problems developed in the first place.

The Credit Repair Organizations Act

The federal Credit Repair Organizations Act (CROA) was signed into law in 1996 to help prevent abuses by credit repair firms and to help consumers make more informed decisions if

W A R N I N G

If a creditor or a collection agency accepts the terms of your check for partial payment of a past due debt, you have no guarantee that the company will actually stop trying to collect from you or that the negative information will be removed from your credit file.

they want help rebuilding their credit. The law is enforced by the FTC.

Here are some of the key provisions of the CROA regarding firms that promise to repair/rebuild your credit record.

- The firm must provide you with a written contract that details the services it will provide. The contract must also indicate the total cost of its services and indicate how long it will take to achieve results, spell out any guarantees the firm makes, and provide its name and business address.
- After signing the contract, you have the right to cancel it for any reason within three business days. However, to cancel, you must fill out and return the form that you should have received with the contract.
- The firm may not provide you with any of the services you have contracted for until after the three-day cancellation period is up.
- The firm may not take money from you or charge you in any way until it has provided you with all of the services spelled out in its contract.
- Before providing you with a written contract or statement, the firm must give you a *Consumer Credit File Rights under State and Federal Law* disclosure statement. The CROA spells out exactly how the statement must be worded. Among other things, the statement must inform you of your right to dispute inaccurate or out-of-date credit record information on your own and your right to obtain a copy of your credit record from the credit bureaus. In addition, the statement must provide you with an overview of your rights when you are working with a credit repair firm, including the right to sue if the firm violates the CROA.
- The firm may not make any misleading statements to you, provide you with misleading advice, or attempt to deceive you in any way.
- The firm may not encourage you to alter your identity in order to get a new, problem-free credit identity.

> # H O T   T I P
>
> The FTC's Telemarketing Sales Rule forbids telemarketers who sell credit repair services from requiring consumers to pay them until their services have been completed.

Legal Remedies under the CROA

Credit repair firms that violate the CROA face stiff penalties. For example, contracts that don't comply with the law are void and unenforceable. Furthermore, consumers can sue any credit repair firm that violates the CROA for actual damages, or the amount they paid to the firm, whichever is larger. They can also sue for whatever punitive damages the court allows and for court costs and attorney fees. The CROA also permits class action lawsuits.

State Restrictions

In addition to federal legislation, at the time this book was revised, some 39 states in addition to the District of Columbia had enacted legislation regulating credit repair firms. A list of these states appears in Figure 6.2. The provisions of the state laws tend to be similar to those of the CROA. Call your state attorney general's office of consumer protection for information about the law in your state. If your state is not listed in Figure 6.2, call your state attorney general's office to find out if a credit repair law was passed since this book was revised.

FIGURE 6.2
States with Legislation Controlling the Actions of Credit Repair Firms

In addition to the District of Columbia, states that have passed legislation to control the activities and business practices of credit repair firms include the following:

Arizona	Kansas	North Carolina
Arkansas	Louisiana	Ohio
California	Maine	Oklahoma
Colorado	Maryland	Oregon
Connecticut	Massachusetts	Pennsylvania
Delaware	Michigan	Tennessee
Florida	Minnesota	Texas
Georgia	Missouri	Utah
Hawaii	Nebraska	Virginia
Idaho	Nevada	Washington
Illinois	New Hampshire	West Virginia
Indiana	New Jersey	Wisconsin
Iowa	New York	

How to Find a Reputable Firm to Help You Rebuild Your Credit

You may want professional help resolving a problem in your credit record or rebuilding your credit record. Maybe you don't have the time to do it yourself or you feel unsure of your ability to do it on your own. Here is how to tell if a credit repair firm is reputable or not:

- Call your state attorney general's office to find out if there have been any complaints or legal actions taken against the firm.
- Check out the credit repair firm with your local better business bureau.

- Avoid firms that do not comply with the requirements of the CROA, which were summarized earlier in this chapter.
- Make sure that the firm's plan of action is based on the information in your credit file and ask the firm to state in writing what it can and cannot do to improve your credit record.
- Avoid companies that make money-back guarantees. Usually, those guarantees are little more than ploys to get your money and run.
- Steer clear of firms that do not tell you about your legal rights and advise you about what you can do yourself for free.

What to Do If You Are Ripped Off

If you are victimized by a credit repair firm, do the following right away:

- Contact your state attorney general's office if your state has a credit repair law. You may be able to use it to get back some or all of your money.
- Meet with a consumer law attorney who has specific experience prosecuting credit repair firms to discuss whether you have a good case. If you do and you win your law-

WARNING

Do not sign a contract with a firm that promises to repair/rebuild your credit record unless you have read it thoroughly and are 100 percent sure that you understand everything in it.

suit, you can recover actual damages or the amount you actually paid to the credit repair firm (whichever is greater), whatever additional punitive damages the court allows, your legal costs, and your attorney fees. Use the resources described in Chapter 4 to find a good attorney.

- Register a complaint about the firm with your local better business bureau if the firm is locally based.
- File a complaint against the firm with the National Fraud Information Center (NFIC) if the firm marketed its services to you via the Web or through telemarketing. You can file your complaint by calling 800-876-7060 or by going to <www.fraud.org>.
- File a complaint with the FTC. Filing a complaint could help prevent other consumers from getting ripped off like you did. To file a complaint, go to <www.ftc.gov>, call 877-382-4357, or write to the FTC at: Federal Trade Commission, Consumer Response Center, 600 Pennsylvania Avenue, NW, Washington, DC 20580.

CHAPTER

7

Women and Credit

The daughter of a long-time client came to me for advice. Sandra C. had just started college and had received several credit card offers through the mail. She was a bright young woman who had watched her parents go through difficult financial times because they had used credit too much. She wanted to avoid having similar problems while she was in college and after graduation.

Sandra was full of questions. She wanted to know how to build and maintain a good credit history and whether she would have to make any changes in her credit accounts if she got married. Sandra also wanted to know about mistakes women tend to make when it comes to credit and what she should do to avoid making them. She also asked if any federal laws applied to women and credit.

Sandra is unique because she actively sought out information about credit. Too many of my female clients (and my male clients) don't seek out information until they are having problems because their marital status has changed—sometimes very unexpectedly—because of a divorce or the death of their spouse. As I explained to Sandra, to avoid such problems, it is imperative that all women get educated about credit and money management and that they establish and maintain their own credit identities separate from their husband's. I also told Sandra that single women with established credit histories should maintain their own credit identities after they marry and that married women who share their husband's credit should build a credit history in their own name with as few ties as possible to their husband's credit.

In this chapter, I discuss why women often have difficulty establishing a credit history of their own, provide an overview of some of the credit-related issues women commonly face, and talk about the best way to deal with those issues. Special issues related to credit and divorce are discussed in Chapter 8.

Why Many Women Have Problems with Credit

When women do not have a credit identity of their own, they are apt to have problems if they experience a change in their marital status as a result of divorce or widowhood. Their problems tend to be the result of several factors.

- Traditionally, women have taken their husband's names and relied on them to handle money matters, including applying for credit cards and loans. As a result, many women do not have credit in their own names.
- Traditionally, women have not understood why they should have a credit history completely separate from their husband's credit record.
- Despite advances in pay equity over the past 30-plus years, women still do not earn as much as men.

In the past, most women did not work outside the home, and consumer credit was acquired and maintained in their husband's name only, not in their own name or in the names of both spouses. Although many women helped manage their family's finances—and some women earned money to help pay the bills—most never developed their own credit identities. As a result, these women were financial nonentities in the eyes of creditors and the credit reporting industry.

Today, two-income households are the norm rather than the exception. Many women, however, like consumers in general, remain relatively uninformed about credit, credit bureaus, and the credit reporting process. Furthermore, they tend not to appreciate why having credit in their own name is important. Therefore, many women do not.

Women cannot afford to remain financially naive and vulnerable in a society in which they often allow their careers to take a back seat to their marriages and interrupt their careers to raise a family, where wives tend to outlive their husbands, and an estimated 50 percent of all marriages end in divorce. Therefore, it is essential that women know how to manage their own finances whether they are single, married, widowed, or divorced. Married women in particular need to actively participate in the management of their family's finances and maintain their own credit identity.

Learning about Credit and Money Management

If you are a woman, there are many ways to educate yourself about money matters. Examples include the following:

- *Take a money management class at your local community college or university.* The extension division of some state universities, in cooperation with the American Association of Retired Persons, offers a Women's Financial Information Program to help middle-aged and older women develop money management skills and help build the confidence to make decisions about their finances.
- *Contact your local Consumer Credit Counseling Services office.* Find out if it offers courses on money management and using credit.
- *Go to your local library or bookstore for books and magazines on personal finance.*
- *Visit money management Web sites.* A good one is <www.bankrate.com>.

- *Visit financial education Web sites just for women.* See <www.wife.org> and <www.ivillage.com/money>.
- *Contact your local college, university, and public school system.* Find out if they offer continuing education or adult education courses related to credit and money.

The Significance of Account-User Status Designations

An important but often overlooked part of credit education is understanding the meaning of common account-user status designations and why some designations are better than others when you want to build a credit record in your own name.

Account-user status designations indicate to creditors and potential creditors the person or persons who can use a particular account and the degree to which each user is legally responsible for managing that account. Generally, when you apply for credit, you establish who can use the credit and who will have responsibility for paying the credit balances, although you may be able to add another user at a later date. Being listed as an authorized user on your husband's accounts will do little to help you build your own credit history. Also, if all of your accounts are joint accounts—accounts that your share with your husband—you may lose that credit if you become separated, divorced, or widowed.

The most common account-user designations and their effects on your credit-building efforts are summarized below.

- *Authorized-user status.* If you are listed as an authorized user on your husband's account, you have permission to use the account but no legal responsibility for paying it. In other words, authorized-user status indicates that you are relying on your spouse's earning power to make payments on the account. Accounts with this status are of minimal value when you are trying to establish your own credit history.
- *Joint-user status.* If you have joint-user status on an account, you and your husband can both use the account,

and you share equal legal responsibility for account payments. Because there is shared responsibility, joint-user accounts can help you build your own credit history. However, these accounts also link your credit history to your husband's, which means that if he abuses a joint credit account, the adverse account information will appear in your credit history as well as his. In other words, his actions can damage your credit record.

- *Individual.* If your account is designated as individual, you qualified for the credit on your own, without your husband. Therefore, you have responsibility for paying on the account, and you are the only person authorized to use the account. Therefore, individual accounts put you in the best position if your marital status changes, because they do not link your use of credit or your ability to obtain credit to your spouse's income and credit history.

Women Living in Community Property States

If you live in a community property state, you should realize that you will not necessarily enjoy the benefits of individual credit and that it will be harder for you to insulate yourself from any money troubles that your husband or former husband may have. Community property states are Arizona, California, Idaho, Louisiana, Nevada, New Mexico, Texas, Washington, and Wisconsin. The Commonwealth of Puerto Rico also has community property laws.

In community property states, husbands and wives are viewed as economic partners, and the after-marriage earnings and property of each spouse are considered to be jointly held and controlled. Therefore, if you live in a community property state, and your spouse gets credit in his own name during your marriage and then does not pay the debt, and the creditor sues your husband and wins the lawsuit, it can try to collect its judgment from any of your marital assets (the community property you earned or acquired during your marriage), regardless of who bought or uses them.

When you apply for credit in your own name in a community property state, the creditor can ask you about your marital status and request information about your husband—if he will be contractually liable for the debt or if you are relying on his income to help make the account payments. However, if half of your community property and income (in community property states, each spouse owns half of the value of their marital assets) qualifies you for the credit you are applying for, your husband will not have to be a coapplicant. The creditor will still have the right to ask you information about him, however.

If you are living in a community property state and you use property that is jointly owned by you and your husband as collateral for a loan, the creditor can require your husband to cosign for the loan, even if only you not you and your spouse, will make the loan payments. Your husband cannot be required to be a cosignor on the note unless he will be specifically obligated to help repay the debt.

Women and Credit in Separate Property States

Most states are separate property states. In these states, the credit history of a woman's husband is irrelevant to her request for credit because, by law, she alone is responsible for making payments on the debts she incurs in her own name. Also, in these states, a husband is not required to cosign a credit application, and creditors are barred from asking a woman about her marital status.

There are exceptions, however. For example, when a woman wants to finance the purchase of real estate in her own name, the creditor can require that her spouse cosign the note. (The same would hold true if her husband purchased real estate in his own name.) By having the spouse cosign on a mortgage, the creditor is ensuring that if one spouse defaults on the loan, it can take the collateral and sell it to recover its costs. For specific information about marital property rights in your state, contact your state's attorney general office.

The Advantage of Individual Credit

Having good individual credit gives you a couple important benefits both in and out of marriage. First, if your husband experiences financial difficulty and has trouble paying his bills, or if he is a poor money manager and doesn't pay his accounts on time, the good credit you have in your own name will remain unblemished even though his is damaged. This would not be the case if you and your spouse shared all of the accounts he was not paying on time.

Second, with your own credit, you will be in a better position to maximize your family's financial options and opportunities—a fact that would be especially important if your spouse got into financial trouble, lost his job, or became seriously ill and had to stop working. In such situations, you will be able to

---

HOT TIP

Married women should have their own bank accounts as well as their own credit. Not only will having money in a separate bank account help them build their own credit histories, but it will also help them get loans in their own names. Also, if a woman's spouse is irresponsible with money, she can use her account to help manage her family's finances and won't have to worry that he may squander the money in their shared account, leaving her without enough money to pay their bills.

offer your family more alternatives for dealing with any financial problems.

Third, as discussed earlier, when you have your own credit identity, you will be in a better position to create a positive life for yourself should you become separated, divorced, or widowed.

If you are married and are in the process of building your own credit history, your ultimate goal should be to qualify for individual credit in your own name and to keep your joint credit to an absolute minimum. But, if you have little or no individual credit right now, you may need to begin the credit building effort by applying for joint credit. Then, once you and your spouse have established a good payment history on those accounts, you can use that history to help qualify for individual credit. However, this is not a good approach if you are concerned that your husband may abuse the credit you share together, damaging his credit history and yours. View shared or joint credit only as a means to an end—obtaining individual credit.

How to Build Your Own Credit History

There is no single, surefire way to develop a credit history for yourself, but the approach outlined in this section is an excel-

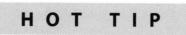

H O T   T I P

If your ex-spouse assumes responsibility for paying off your joint accounts as part of your divorce agreement and then does not live up to the agreement, the unpaid creditors have the right to look to you for their money. This is another key argument for why individual credit is better than joint credit.

lent way to begin. It starts with the easiest types of credit to qualify for and builds to credit that is more difficult to obtain.

Before you begin the credit-building process, make sure that any assets owned by you and your husband—your home, cars, stocks and mutual funds, bank accounts, and so on—are listed in both of your names. Then, whenever you apply for credit and are asked to list your assets, you can include all of them.

Request a copy of your credit report and your husband's from each of the big three credit bureaus before you begin the credit application process. That way, you can find out which, if any, of them are maintaining a credit file on you and what is in each of those files. When you receive copies of your credit reports, review them carefully for errors and omissions. If you find any, follow the steps outlined in Chapter 4 for correcting credit record problems.

If all of your credit is in your husband's name, you can ask each of the credit bureaus that is maintaining a credit file on him to establish a file in your name, too. Your credit file should include any accounts you set up in your own name, accounts in your husband's name that you use as an authorized user, and accounts in your husband's name that you are contractually liable for (applicable only if you live in a community property state). In addition, ask creditors to begin reporting credit information in your name as well as your husband's.

Once you have a credit record in your own name, you may want to use joint accounts to help build your history. Make sure the accounts are included in your credit record, assuming they have positive payment histories. Also, make sure that any credit you had in your maiden name is part of your credit record. If you find that some of those accounts are missing, write to the appropriate credit bureau and ask that the information be added.

Once you have reviewed your credit reports and those of your spouse and dealt with any problems, you are ready to start the credit-building process. If you have little or no credit, obtain a small, cash-secured loan from your bank. This step is important, because if your marital situation changes in the future and you need to borrow money, you will already have a relationship with the bank.

To obtain a loan, schedule an appointment with a loan officer and explain what you are trying to accomplish. Make sure that the bank will report your loan payment history to at least one of the three national credit bureaus. If the first bank you talk with won't make your loan, go to another bank. When you find one that is willing to work with you, open a checking account or a savings account in your own name at that bank.

The bank will give you either an unsecured or a secured loan. If it asks you to secure the loan, it may let you do that with one of your assets—your car for example—or you may have to collateralize the loan by purchasing a certificate of deposit (CD) with the loan proceeds. If you do the latter, you will not have use of the money you borrow. This should not be a problem for you, however, because the purpose of the loan is to help you build a solid credit history in your own name, not to purchase things.

If you default on the loan, the bank will collect what it is owed by taking the money from your certificate of deposit or by taking the asset you posted as collateral. Once you've paid off the loan, order another copy of your credit report so that you can be sure that it accurately reflects your loan payments.

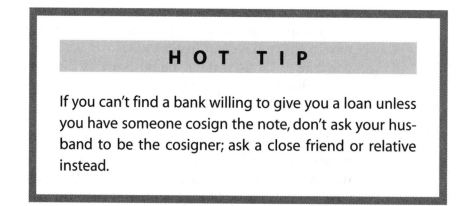

HOT TIP

If you can't find a bank willing to give you a loan unless you have someone cosign the note, don't ask your husband to be the cosigner; ask a close friend or relative instead.

Depending on your situation, after you have paid off your loan, you may be ready to obtain a national bank card in your own name, or you may need to apply for a second loan. Ideally this second loan will be unsecured, and you will not need a cosigner.

If you are approved for a national bank card, charge small amounts at a time and make your payments on time. Chapter 11 in this book explains how to shop for a national bank card.

If you can't qualify for a national bank card with reasonable terms of credit, you can probably qualify for a secured bank card with good terms. Secured cards are discussed in the next section of this chapter. You may also want to apply for a retail store charge card or an oil and gas card because these types of credit tend to be easy to obtain. Then, once you have a good payment history on those cards, you can apply again for a national bank card. You may have better luck qualifying for one this time.

Secured Bank Cards

If you can't get a national bank card, apply for a secured bank card, which is specifically designed for people who can't qualify for an unsecured MasterCard or Visa. A secured bank card is often used as a stepping stone to an unsecured card and it looks exactly like a regular national bank card.

If you are approved for a secured card, the bank that issues you the card will require that you collateralize your credit purchases, either by opening a savings account with the bank or by purchasing a CD from it. Then, if you default on your account payments, the bank can withdraw money from your account—or cash in your CD—to pay your account balance.

When you shop for a secured bank card, you should consider several factors to get the best deal. They include how much money you must deposit in a savings account with the card issuer or the size of the CD you must purchase; the rate of interest your money will earn at the bank; how much you can charge, as a percentage of your deposit; whether you can con-

> # H O T   T I P
>
> Check out <www.bankrate.com> and/or <www.cardtrak
> .com> for the best deals on secured as well as unse-
> cured bank cards.

vert the secured card to an unsecured card, assuming you make
your secured card payments on time; and the size of the card application fee.

If you already have some credit in your own name, or if you
and your husband have some long-standing, well-performing,
joint credit accounts, you may be able to shorten the credit-
building process, especially if you have a well-paying, relatively
secure job. In such a situation, credit building may simply be a
matter of making sure that you have a bank account, at least one
oil and gas card, and a national bank card. You may also want to
have a travel and entertainment card such as American Express
in your name.

During the credit-building process, use your full name
when you apply for credit, not your husband's name. For example, list your name as Ms. or Mrs. Susan J. Smith, not Mrs. John
Smith. You should also review the credit cards that you already
have to see if any of them are in your husband's name. If you
find any, the information for that account is being reported in
your husband's name and, therefore, it is not helping you build
your own credit history. You have two options in this case, assuming the account is in good standing. One option is to ask
your husband to contact the creditor and request that you be
listed as a joint user on the account and that it issue you a new
card in your own name. The other option is for you to apply for
individual credit with that same creditor. The best option for
you will depend on where you are in the credit-building process.

Additional Credit-Building Advice

As you build your own credit history, be sure to limit the amount of credit you apply for. As already indicated, creditors don't look favorably on consumers with a lot of inquiries in their credit histories. They may worry that you are applying for more credit than you can handle. Also, creditors will not like the fact that you have a lot of credit accounts, even if most of the accounts have zero balances. They know that you could run up the balances on those accounts, and then you might not be able to afford to make your account payments.

Finally, use the credit you obtain to purchase necessities only, not frivolous items, and keep your account balances as low as possible. Be sure to make all account payments on time so that the credit history you build will be a positive one.

The Equal Credit Opportunity Act

When you are building your own credit history, it's important to know about the federal Equal Credit Opportunity Act (ECOA). Enacted in 1974, the ECOA was written to help ensure, among other things, that women are not denied access to credit simply because of their gender. The ECOA also helps married women develop their own credit histories. Figure 7.1 reviews the law's key provisions.

Before the ECOA, most women, regardless of their marital status, had trouble obtaining credit, and therefore, it was difficult, if not impossible, for them to establish their own credit histories. Women were in this situation because men were the breadwinners in most households, and credit and money management topics were not subjects that society felt women needed to know about. Even when a woman chose to work after marriage, creditors assumed that, ultimately, marriage, childbirth, and family responsibilities would interrupt her career and affect her ability to pay her bills. Therefore, women, even women with jobs outside the home, were considered poor credit risks, and most of the credit women used was in their husbands' names. Further-

FIGURE 7.1
Provisions of the ECOA of Special Interest to Women

- Creditors may not discriminate on the basis of race, color, religion, sex, national origin, or marital status.

- A woman may apply for credit under her married name, maiden name, or a combination.

- Creditors must judge the merits of a woman's request for credit based on her earnings and her credit history. Creditors cannot require a husband to cosign an unsecured note for his wife. However, if a woman applies for a secured loan—a car loan or a home mortgage, for example—the lender can require her spouse to sign the legal document that describes the property's legal ownership. The lender cannot require the woman's spouse to cosign the bank note if the woman qualifies for the loan based on her own information. This ECOA provision does not apply in community property states.

- When a woman applies for credit, the creditor may not ask for information about her husband. An important exception to this provision applies to women who rely on alimony or child support to qualify for credit.

- All of a woman's income—including income from part-time work, public assistance, child support, and alimony—must be considered when a creditor evaluates her application for credit. However, the creditor can consider the reliability of the income.

- Women who apply for secured credit can be required to indicate whether they are married, separated, or single. However, a woman's marital status cannot be used to deny her credit or to limit the amount of credit she can have.

- Creditors may not ask a woman to indicate her sex on a credit application unless it is for a home loan, and then only for government reporting purposes.

- If a woman is applying for unsecured credit in her own name, a creditor may not ask her to indicate her marital status unless she lives in a community property state.

FIGURE 7.1
Provisions of the ECOA of Special Interest to Women, continued

- Creditors may not ask about a woman's birth control practices or if she plans to have children, nor may they make assumptions about such matters.

- Although creditors may ask a woman if she has a home phone, they may not ask whether the phone is in her name, because many home telephones are listed in the husband's name.

---

more, even if a woman's name was on a credit account that she actively used, payment history information for that account was reported to credit bureaus in her husband's name only.

To help women develop their own credit histories, the ECOA requires that creditors report account payment data in the names of both spouses on any accounts that they both use or are both liable for. Therefore, if you are a joint user or an authorized user on an account, payment information for that account should appear in your husband's credit file and in yours, assuming the account was opened after June 1, 1977.

Sometimes, creditors disregard this ECOA requirement. Therefore, if you feel that having shared account information, especially joint-user account information, in your credit record will be helpful to your efforts to obtain credit in your own name, contact each of the major credit bureaus to request a copy of your credit record. Request a copy of your husband's, too, assuming you have his permission. Then compare both sets of credit reports to determine if any creditors are reporting information on accounts opened after June 1, 1977, in your husband's name only.

If you discover that an account with a positive payment history is being reported in your husband's name only, write to the creditor. Explain that the account is a shared account that was opened after June 1, 1977, and ask that the creditor begin reporting account payment information in both of your names. Attach to the letter a copy of your credit report and your husband's, and highlight the relevant account name(s) and number(s). You can model your letter after the one in Figure 7.2. A

FIGURE 7.2
Sample Letter to Creditor Asking It to Report Account Information in Both Spouses' Names

(Date)

(Name and Address of Creditor)

Dear (name of credit manager):

As of June 1, 1977, according to the provisions of the federal ECOA, creditors were to begin reporting account information on authorized-user and joint accounts in the names of both spouses. In reviewing the credit files (name of credit bureau) is maintaining on me, (your name as it appears on your account with the creditor), and on my husband, (your husband's name as it appears on the account), I noted that you are not reporting information in my name for the account that we have with you. The number on that account is #_____. This account was opened after June 1, 1977.

Therefore, I am writing to ask that you begin reporting information for this account in my husband's name and in my name, too. I also ask that you make my (name of credit bureau) credit history reflect the current status of my husband's history as reported by you.

Thank you for your assistance. If you have any questions, you may call me at (area code and telephone number).

Sincerely,

(Signature)

(Your name)

> ## WARNING
>
> Even though one of the goals of the ECOA is to make it easier for women to establish their own credit identity, the law requires credit bureaus to report negative as well as positive account information on authorized-user and joint accounts. Ironically, therefore, this requirement can harm you if your spouse has misused an authorized-user or joint-user account. However, you can try to distance yourself from your husband's mismanagement by preparing a written statement of no more than 100 words explaining the reason(s) for the negative account information. You should also attach a copy of this statement to any applications for credit, insurance, or rental housing you make in your own name. Chapter 4 discusses written statements.

few months later, request copies of your credit reports again to check that the creditor honored your request.

If you and your husband share accounts that were opened before June 1, 1977, and you would like those accounts to be reflected in your credit report, write to each creditor and ask that they start doing so. Although creditors are not legally required to, most will honor your request.

Advice for Women Who Have Credit in Their Own Names and Are Getting Married

If you are one of the countless single, working women who has a positive credit history in her own name, it is important to preserve that good history after you marry. Therefore, when you marry, do not cancel your credit accounts, and be sure to maintain at least one bank account—checking or savings—in your own name. There is no reason to merge all of your finances with your husband's just because of your marriage. Furthermore, it is far easier to maintain an already positive credit history separately from your spouse's than it is to lose that identity and then have to reestablish it. Finally, as this chapter has already pointed out, having your own credit when you are married can be a big help if your family goes through some tough financial times.

If you change your name when you get married, notify your creditors right away and ask them to begin reporting your account information to credit bureaus in your married name. A few months later, request a copy of your credit report from each of the three national credit reporting agencies to make sure that the creditors followed your instructions.

If you marry and have no credit history in your own name, begin immediately to establish one by following the credit-building steps outlined earlier in this chapter.

Advice for Women Who Were Married before the ECOA Was Enacted

If you were married before the ECOA went into effect, if all of your credit is shared with your husband, and if most of that credit was obtained before June 1, 1977, it's very likely that none of the three national credit reporting agencies is maintaining a credit file on you in your name. As a result, establishing your own credit identity will be somewhat more difficult than for married women who are listed as authorized or joint users on accounts that were opened after June 1977. Nonetheless, it can be done.

Your first step should be to order a copy of your credit record from each of the big three so that you will know if you have a credit record with them in your name and what is in those credit records. Get any errors corrected right away following the advice in Chapter 4.

Request copies of your husband's reports, too, if your husband says it's okay. (You should not order someone else's credit report without their cooperation.) You should make certain that your husband's record is problem-free, because you may need to open one or more joint accounts with him as part of your credit-building process.

Talk with your husband about what you are trying to accomplish, and explain why it is important for you to have your own credit. If he doesn't seem to understand and is reluctant to help you get started, suggest that he read this chapter and talk with a Consumer Credit Counseling Services counselor, your family's financial advisor, or your banker.

Once your husband understands why you need your own credit identity, suggest that you apply for some new joint credit together. Because creditors must report the payment information on your new joint credit to credit bureaus in both of your names, the joint credit will get the credit-building process started. However, don't forget that your ultimate goal is to establish credit in just your name, so a credit history based on joint accounts won't be enough.

Widows and Credit

If your husband is ill and you believe that he will not recover, it is important for you to prepare financially for widowhood. This preparation is analogous to what you should do prior to getting divorced.

- Build a credit history for yourself.
- Correct problems in your credit file if you already have one. Do the same for your husband's credit file.
- Prepare written explanations for any adverse information in your credit record (or your spouse's) that is the result of events beyond your control—an illness, a sudden job loss, or your husband's money mismanagement.
- Talk with a financial advisor you trust.

If widowhood happens suddenly and you don't have a credit record in your own name, you'll face a number of financial obstacles that may impede your ability to build a happy and satisfying life on your own. For example, you may not have ready access to credit, and you may also find it difficult to obtain adequate insurance or even a job.

If you were an authorized user on your husband's accounts, his creditors may cancel those accounts once they learn that he has died. In addition, creditors can require that you reapply for credit on joint accounts if the accounts were based on your spouse's income. However, if a joint account was based on your income, or if either of you could have qualified by yourselves for the credit at the time of application, you will probably not have to reapply.

One way to deal with a possible loss of credit is to delay letting creditors know about the death of your spouse. This way, you will have time to get your finances in order and to begin applying for credit in your own name if possible. However, if any of the creditors learn about your spouse's death before you tell them, the fact that you withheld the information could prejudice them against you when you reapply for credit. There is no way for you to know ahead of time if this could happen, so you will have to decide if the risk is worth it or not. In fact, many

HOT TIP

An excellent book about the financial and psychological issues that widows face is *On Your Own: A Widow's Passage to Emotional and Financial Well-Being,* 2nd edition, by Alexandra Armstrong and Mary Donahue (Dearborn Financial Publishing, Inc.).

women continue to use their husband's credit cards long after their spouses have died without any problem. If you choose to do this, however, don't delay building credit in your own name. You will have problems eventually if you want to borrow money to buy a new car, a smaller home, go back to school, remodel your home, and so on.

When you apply for credit after your husband's death (and during any credit reapplication process), potential creditors cannot discount or ignore income you may receive from annuities, pensions, Social Security, and/or disability programs during their decision-making process. However, they can consider the reliability of those payments when deciding whether or not to approve your application.

If you have little or no credit in your own name at the time of your husband's death, start the credit-building process. As you do, remember that the ECOA requires creditors to consider information in your husband's file when you apply for credit, if you can prove that his credit history reflects yours. Although it's a long shot, trying to make that argument can pay off depending on your situation.

Other Considerations

Once your husband dies, any funds in bank accounts that you held jointly with a right of survivorship will go directly to you and will not be tied up in the probate process. The same

---

H O T   T I P

After you are widowed, don't lie when you fill out a credit application by pretending that your husband is still alive. You will be committing a federal crime if you do.

holds true for any life insurance benefits to which you are entitled and other assets owned by your spouse for which you were the designated beneficiary. To receive the insurance policy proceeds, however, you must file a claim, and after you file, you may have to wait a month or more before you actually receive the funds. This delay is an argument for the importance of having credit in your own name. You may need that credit to help pay your expenses while you are waiting for the insurance proceeds and for whatever your husband left to you in his will.

After your husband's death, you may have to pay the debts he leaves behind. Repayment will depend on the nature of those debts, however. For example, you may have to pay the debts you shared with money from your bank accounts, insurance proceeds, or with any other assets that are not part of the probate process. You will also be responsible for any debts owed by your deceased spouse that were secured with property.

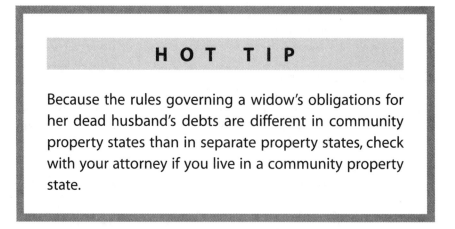

HOT TIP

Because the rules governing a widow's obligations for her dead husband's debts are different in community property states than in separate property states, check with your attorney if you live in a community property state.

Creating
Divorce-Proof Credit

Mary E. was going through a difficult divorce when she came to my office with questions about how the divorce might affect her credit history. She had never been concerned about it before, because throughout their 20-year marriage, her husband had maintained all of their accounts in his name, and whenever they needed new credit, her husband applied for it. She had never anticipated that her marriage would fall apart. In their divorce agreement, Mary's husband had agreed to assume responsibility for paying off the debt they had acquired during their marriage; however, after their divorce was final, her ex-husband's business began to fail—an unexpected consequence of their divorce. Now, Mary was worried about what would happen if her ex-husband did not live up to the terms of their agreement or filed for bankruptcy. She wanted to know if she would be responsible for paying off their marital debts if her husband didn't, which was a problem because her salary barely covered her basic needs. She was concerned that she too might end up in bankruptcy.

As I prepared to give Mary the information and advice she needed, I thought how much better a situation she would be in if she had planned for the possibility that her marriage might not work out and had established her own credit history. If she had, she might not be feeling so vulnerable and worried.

An estimated 50 percent of all American marriages end in divorce. Therefore, many women face problems like Mary's, especially if they did not plan for minimizing the negative financial impact of divorce. In addition, an increasing number of men face problems like Mary's these days, because more women are pursuing successful careers or starting their own businesses and becoming their families' major bread winners. In many households, therefore, the woman's income, not the man's, qualifies couples for joint credit. Therefore, when these couples split up, traditional divorce arrangements may not apply, and it may be the former husband, not the former wife, who experiences financial problems.

No matter how happy your marital relationship and regardless of your gender, it's a good idea to prepare financially for the possibility that your marriage may fail. To help you, this chapter discusses some of the problems both sexes may face after divorce, how to avoid them, and what to do if they develop. The chapter also provides information about divorce and bankruptcy.

Planning for a Divorce

If you are contemplating divorce, you can minimize any potential financial damage by taking certain steps before your divorce begins. These steps include the following:

- Make sure that you have good credit in your own name. If you don't, delay your divorce, if possible, until you can get some credit in your own name. Also, open a bank account in your own name. For advice about building your own credit history, read Chapter 5.
- Know the status of the accounts you and your spouse are currently using. Are they joint, authorized-user, or individual? Is each account current?
- If you already have either joint or individual credit, obtain a copy of your credit report from each of the three

national credit bureaus and address any problems you may find.

- If some of the accounts in your credit reports are joint accounts with negative histories, and if the adverse information is the fault of your soon-to-be former spouse or the result of circumstances beyond your control—loss of a job or an expensive hospitalization, for example—prepare a written explanation. Also, ask the credit bureau that prepared the report containing the negative information to make your explanation a permanent part of your credit history. Your explanation may help disassociate you from the account's problems. It is also a good idea to attach the same explanation to any credit applications you complete.

- Open up your own bank accounts.

- Pay all bills and credit card debts you share with your spouse from your joint funds. Then, send a letter to each creditor canceling those credit accounts. If you leave them open, you risk being liable for the balances on the accounts, even if you did not run them up.

- If you have a lawyer or a financial advisor you trust, talk with that person about how you should prepare for the change in your marital status.

- If your spouse files for bankruptcy while you are in the process of divorce, it is likely that the divorce proceedings will be stopped until the bankruptcy is completed, or the automatic stay will be lifted so that your divorce can proceed. During this time, talk with your lawyer about how to minimize the impact of your spouse's troubles on your financial situation.

Avoiding Trouble with Joint or Shared Accounts

As the previous chapter indicated, creditors consider spouses with joint accounts, including national bank cards, bank loans, debit cards, lines of credit, overdraft checking, and so on, to be equally liable for the balances on those accounts. Therefore, when you are getting divorced, it is critical that you close all joint accounts as soon as possible and reopen new accounts separately in your own name. Authorized-user accounts should also be closed. If you don't close the accounts, you risk being liable for any charges your ex-spouse runs up on them, even if your divorce agreement says your former spouse will be 100 percent responsible for the accounts. As long as your name is still on the accounts, you are legally liable for them regardless of what your divorce agreement says. Furthermore, if your ex-spouse does not pay your joint accounts on time or defaults on those accounts, your credit record as well as his or hers will be damaged, which could hamper your ability to build a life for yourself as a single person.

To close a joint or authorized-user account, write to the creditor. If the balance is outstanding on any of these accounts, ask that it be transferred to the new individual account of whichever spouse will be responsible for paying off the debt according to the terms of your divorce agreement. Also, in your letter ask that the spouse who is *not* responsible for the account be released from liability for it. Although the creditor is not obligated to comply with your request, it is important that both you

HOT TIP

If at all possible, avoid a divorce agreement that allows your spouse to maintain your joint accounts in exchange for paying off their outstanding balances. As long as those joint accounts remain open—whether you use them or not—you will be legally liable for them, regardless of what your divorce agreement says.

> # HOT TIP
>
> While your joint accounts are still open, keep all account payments up-to-date, even if your spouse is no longer paying them. That way, your credit history will not be damaged.

and your spouse are clear about exactly who will be responsible for each debt after you are divorced.

If you want to close a joint account and apply for new, individual credit with the same creditor, the creditor has the right to require you to reapply for the credit if the joint account was based on the income of your spouse. However, if it was based on your income, or if either of you could have qualified for the credit at the time of application, the creditor probably won't make you reapply.

Debts That Your Spouse Agrees to Pay as Part of Your Divorce Settlement

When you and your spouse decide to get divorced, part of your divorce negotiations will involve deciding how to divide your marital debts as well as your marital assets. Those decisions should be clearly stated in your divorce agreement. Be sure to send a letter to each of the creditors affected by your agreement notifying them of what you and your spouse have decided.

After you are divorced, each of you will be expected to pay off the debts for which you agreed to be responsible. However, if your spouse fails to pay a particular creditor, the creditor can seek payment from you, if your name was on the account when the debt was first incurred.

> ## HOT TIP
>
> If your former spouse violates the terms of your divorce agreement, talk with your divorce attorney about whether legal action is appropriate.

Other Credit Problems Divorce Can Create

If you get divorced and don't already have credit in your own name, you'll be in a very vulnerable position. For example, as this chapter has explained, if you and your ex-spouse agree to keep certain joint accounts open so that you'll have access to credit and if you both use those accounts, you'll each be equally liable for paying them. This shared liability could spell disaster if your former spouse runs up a big account balance and cannot or will not help with the payments. On the other hand, if you and your spouse close all of your joint accounts as part of your divorce, or if your spouse removes you as an authorized user on his or her individual accounts, then when your marriage ends, you may be left without any access to credit. Not having credit could make your efforts to establish a new life for yourself as a single person an uphill battle.

As Chapter 7 noted, creditors may not deny a consumer continued use of accounts shared with a former spouse, nor may they change the terms of credit simply because of a change in marital status. They may, however, require that you reapply for the credit in your own name and based on your own finances. Therefore, in marriages where a significant earnings disparity exists between spouses and where the spouse with the smaller income shared accounts with the other, the person who earns less risks losing the credit.

If you reapply for credit that was once joint or if you apply for completely new credit, creditors are prohibited from discounting or refusing to consider any child support, maintenance, or alimony you receive as well as any other unearned income. However, as previously noted, they are allowed to consider the reliability of these income sources, and they can deny you credit if they judge them to be unreliable and you need the unearned income to qualify for the credit. Therefore, if unearned income is important to your future creditworthiness, it's a good idea to collect and save any documentation you may have that supports its reliability. The documentation might include your divorce agreement, a notarized letter from your ex-spouse, canceled checks, your IRS tax returns, and your bank statements.

When they evaluate your creditworthiness, creditors must consider the credit history of your former spouse, if you can demonstrate that it reflects your history, too. If it is a positive history and if you have no credit in your own name and never shared credit with your former spouse, you may want to try to make this case to help build your own credit history. However, there is no guarantee that your spouse's credit history will help you. Copies of checks you wrote to pay the accounts of your former spouse while you were married, letters you may have written to creditors regarding the accounts, and so on could help

H O T   T I P

If you take back your maiden name after your divorce, be certain to let your creditors know, and ask them to begin reporting account information to credit bureaus in your new name. Then wait a few months and check your credit record again to make sure that it is happening.

demonstrate to potential creditors that your former spouse's history reflects yours. If you are on good terms with your former spouse, he or she may even be willing to write a letter to a potential creditor attesting to the fact that you regularly used the accounts and helped manage them.

If Your Former Spouse Files for Bankruptcy

In today's economy, it's possible that your former spouse may file for bankruptcy. Even though the bankruptcy may erase any debt that your former spouse owes you as part of your divorce agreement, it will not cancel any obligations to pay you alimony, maintenance, or child support, nor will it wipe out most tax debts. They will continue to be the legal obligations of your former spouse.

If your former spouse files for Chapter 13 bankruptcy (reorganization of debt), he or she will have to prepare a reorganization plan. Among other things, the plan will spell out what your ex intends to do about all of the money he or she owes, including the alimony, maintenance, and/or child support payments you have not been paid.

If your former spouse is behind on alimony, maintenance, or child support payments and files a Chapter 7 bankruptcy (liquidation of debt), you may not be able to collect any of the past due payments you are entitled to until the bankruptcy is over

---

H O T T I P

Alimony, maintenance, and child support obligations have priority in a bankruptcy. Those obligations must be paid before tax debts and before most unsecured debts.

> ## HOT TIP
>
> If you think that your ex-spouse may be getting ready to file for bankruptcy and he or she is paying you alimony, maintenance, or child support, consult with a bankruptcy attorney right away.

and the court lifts the automatic stay. An automatic stay is a court action that prohibits most but not all creditor collection actions against a debtor once the debtor has filed for bankruptcy. The automatic stay ends either when a bankruptcy is over or when the court lifts or removes the stay. Despite the automatic stay, however, while your former spouse is in bankruptcy, he or she must make all current alimony, maintenance, and child support payments on time. That obligation continues. The bankruptcy only affects past due obligations.

One option to consider if your former spouse files a Chapter 7 and owes you money is to try to collect the debt from the assets that are not part of your ex-spouse's bankruptcy estate while the bankruptcy is ongoing. These assets are called *exempt assets,* and an automatic stay does not affect them. Talk with a consumer bankruptcy attorney in your area about collecting from the exempt assets of your former spouse.

Two important exceptions to the bankruptcy provision prevent your ex-spouse from using bankruptcy to get rid of the legal obligation to pay alimony, maintenance, and/or child support according to the terms of your divorce agreement. The first exception exists if your ex-spouse falls behind on any of those payments and you voluntarily turn over the past due payments to a collection agency or an attorney who collects debts as a regular part of his or her practice. If you do, the bankruptcy court can wipe out the past due alimony, maintenance, and/or child support payments. However, your ex-spouse will be legally obligated to make all future payments to you in full and on time.

The second exception occurs if your former spouse asks the court to rule that a debt that is classified as child support, alimony, or maintenance is really another type of debt related to the change in his or her marital status—a property settlement obligation, for example—and should, therefore, be discharged. If the court agrees with your ex, no matter what kind of bankruptcy your former spouse has filed, the debt will be wiped out.

Property Settlement and Hold Harmless Obligations

Until 1994, if your divorce agreement allowed your ex-spouse to keep a particular asset in exchange for promising to pay you a set amount of money or to pay off some of your debts, your ex-spouse could use bankruptcy to wipe out those obligations. The same used to be true if your divorce agreement provided that you would accept smaller alimony, maintenance, or child support payments in exchange for being "held harmless" (i.e., not liable) for certain debts that you incurred during your marriage. As a result, you could be left with a lot of debt and little or no alimony, support, or maintenance income to help you pay that debt, which might force you into bankruptcy.

The 1994 Bankruptcy Code was amended to change the way that divorce-related property settlements and hold harmless agreements must be treated in bankruptcy. Now, as a result, a bankruptcy will not necessarily release your former spouse from property settlement and hold harmless obligations, assuming the court decides that your former spouse has enough resources to pay you alimony, maintenance, and/or child support and his or her own basic living expenses as well. If your former spouse can prove that he or she cannot do that, all or some of the property settlement and hold harmless obligations in your divorce will be discharged. They will also be discharged if your ex-spouse is a business owner and can prove to the court that making those payments will not leave enough money to continue the business. However, your former spouse's property settlement and hold harmless obligations will not be erased if the court believes that doing so would cause you more harm than the potential benefits your former spouse might enjoy.

There is an important catch to these exceptions, however: To benefit from them, you must file an adversary proceeding—the equivalent of a mini-lawsuit—against your ex-spouse within 60 days of the date of the first creditor's meeting in the bankruptcy. For you to do that, you must know that your former spouse has filed for bankruptcy, know the date of the first creditor's meeting, and have sufficient financial resources to hire an attorney who can help you, because it's not advisable to initiate an adversary proceeding yourself.

Other Aspects of Bankruptcy Law That May Affect You If You Are Divorced

You should know about some other aspects of the federal bankruptcy code if you want to receive child support; if you want to modify an existing order for alimony, maintenance, or support; or if you placed a lien on property owned by your former spouse as part of your property settlement agreement. Each of these issues is highlighted in this section. If you want additional information about them, speak with your divorce attorney or with a consumer bankruptcy attorney.

- A bankruptcy cannot affect any actions necessary to establish the paternity of a child. Therefore, if you have to establish the paternity of your child to get your state attorney general's office to help you get child support, your efforts can continue if the man files for bankruptcy. If he is subsequently identified as the father of your child, he will have to begin making child support payments, despite the fact that he has filed for bankruptcy.

- If you want to establish or modify an order for alimony, maintenance, or support and your ex-spouse is in bankruptcy, you can do so without getting the bankruptcy court's permission first. In the past, having to get permission first often created expense, delay, and even hardship for the ex-spouse who wanted the change.

- If you placed a lien on property your former spouse owns to secure a promise in your property agreement that he or she would pay off certain debts that you owe, your ex cannot erase that obligation by filing for bankruptcy.

Special Concerns for Divorced People in Community Property States

If you live in a community property state and are getting a divorce, you will face special problems. Arizona, California, Idaho, Louisiana, Nevada, New Mexico, Texas, Washington, and Wisconsin are all community property states. In these states, both spouses are jointly liable for all debts incurred during their marriage—their individual as well as their joint debts. (In separate property states, this mutual obligation applies only to joint debt.) Therefore, if your former spouse agreed in your divorce agreement to pay off certain individual debts that you incurred during your marriage and then does not live up to the agreement, and if you live in a community property state, the affected creditors can look to you for their money. Otherwise, they can look only to the property accumulated during your marriage to settle their claims.

You have several options if the creditors *do* seek you out. One option is to pay the debt in full to minimize any damage that it will do to your credit history. If you want to pay off the debt but your financial resources are limited, try negotiating a new, more affordable debt payment schedule with the creditors. To initiate those negotiations, contact the creditors by letter, telephone, or in person. Explain your situation, and let them know that you want to pay off your debts but that you need to be able to make smaller monthly payments to do so. If you don't feel comfortable handling the negotiations yourself, the Con-

---

HOT TIP

To learn more about consumer bankruptcy and how the process works, read *The Bankruptcy Kit* by John Ventura (Dearborn Financial Publishing, Inc.). You can purchase the book at a neighborhood bookstore, online, or by calling 800-245-BOOK (2665).

---

sumer Credit Counseling Service (CCCS) office nearest you (800-388-2227) can help for little or no cost.

Another option is to file for bankruptcy, but don't file without speaking with an experienced bankruptcy attorney first and giving this option a lot of serious thought. The attorney will help you understand all the ramifications of bankruptcy. For example, you will learn that having a bankruptcy in your credit record will make it more difficult for you to build a financial life for yourself after a divorce, because the bankruptcy can stay there for up to ten years. During this time, reputable creditors may be reluctant to give you credit at reasonable terms. The attorney should also explore other steps short of bankruptcy for dealing with your money troubles.

WARNING

Bankruptcy is a complicated legal process. Don't try to handle your own. To fully benefit from bankruptcy, hire an experienced consumer bankruptcy attorney.

CHAPTER 9

Privacy Issues in a High-Tech World

Jack Tolifer, an old friend of mine, called me at home one night frustrated and upset. He had just had his dinner interrupted by a telemarketer trying to sell him an investment opportunity, and during their brief conversation, it had become obvious to Jack that the telemarketer knew a good bit about him. Jack was really disturbed by the phone call, so he called me to find out if I had any suggestions for how to reduce the number of telemarketing calls and amount of junk mail he was receiving. He also wanted to know how the telemarketer could have learned so much about him. Jack felt as though his privacy had been violated.

I commiserated with Jack because I had experienced the same problem, but I had taken steps to deal with those annoyances. So I shared with Jack what he could do to reduce telemarketing calls and junk mail. We also talked about the issue of privacy. I explained that through the use of sophisticated technology, companies amass and store detailed data on consumers in their databases and that many of those companies make lots of money off of that information. I warned Jack that there have been instances of individuals who have gained illegal access to this information, and I cautioned him to be more careful with whom he shared information about his personal life, buying habits, and finances.

I hope that after reading this chapter, you will become as concerned about your privacy as Jack and as vigilant as he is now about preserving it. Protecting your privacy is particularly important in light of the growing incidence of identity theft in this country, which is the subject of the next chapter.

This chapter discusses some of the ways that your privacy is threatened in today's world, namely by credit bureaus and other information brokers, creditors, retailers, and other businesses that use and store consumer information in their computers; direct marketers; government agencies; the medical industry; and even unscrupulous individuals. New York Congressman Charles Schumer, before the House Subcommittee on Consumer Affairs and Coinage, said:

> In the modern era, one punch of a computer button can instantly deliver to anyone with a terminal more confidential information about an American consumer than a private detective could unearth in a week. As a result of technology, the privacy of American citizens is imperiled more than at any other time in our history. There is fear among other policymakers that the era of "Big Brother is watching you" has arrived, created by a combination of forces in both the public and the private sectors.

Although Congressman Schumer made these comments in 1991, his concerns are even more valid today, given that the Internet has provided new ways to access and use information about consumers.

This chapter also discusses some of the federal laws that have been passed to help protect your personal and financial information, and it highlights their weaknesses. In the next chapter, you will learn about specific steps you can take to help preserve the privacy of your information.

Privacy in the Information Age

Many marketing databases sell all kinds of information about you to companies, to government agencies, and even, sometimes, to crooks. This information can be as diverse as your in-store and credit card purchases, general buying habits, your medical history, your employment background, information about injuries you may have suffered on the job, records of your telephone calls, information about your home, your household income, marital status, political leanings, and more. Presently, it is perfectly legal in most instances for businesses to create databases that contain such information and sell it to other businesses and to individuals. Many of the databases are not expensive and can be purchased over the Internet with a credit card.

Sometimes, the information in one database is combined with information from another to create new, marketable information products or to improve existing databases. In other cases, information from one database may be compared with that of another to help identify consumers with particular characteristics or to make an existing database more comprehensive

WARNING

Even something as seemingly innocent as a store loyalty card—for example, the grocery store or drug store card that entitles you to discounts on certain items—is used by many retailers to collect information about your shopping habits so they can improve how they market their products and services to you. Some retailers also sell the information they collect using these cards to other businesses.

and accurate. Databases are also linked electronically to create huge information networks.

Despite the fact that our personal information has become a valuable commodity, we are often unaware that information about our finances, personal habits, health, buying patterns, and so on is being bought, sold, and exchanged. Furthermore, although federal laws help limit what businesses can do with our information and give us some control over it, additional legislation is needed.

Unauthorized Access to Your Credit Record Information

In recent years, the three national credit bureaus have made efforts to increase the security of the information in their consumer credit files. However, no security system can be 100 percent foolproof, especially because technology has made it easier for motivated individuals to gain unauthorized access to your credit file, and because online electronic access to credit bureau information has become commonplace. For example, employees at businesses with computer access to credit bureau data—car dealerships, brokerage houses, and local banks for example—may obtain personal and financial information on consumers and then sell the information for big bucks. Also, there have been instances of individuals and unscrupulous businesses who misrepresented themselves in order to access credit record data and of businesses and individuals who had a legitimate reason to access this information but who used it for illegal purposes or sold it to others. Although amendments to the FCRA have tried to tighten controls on who can access credit record data, there is no reason to think that the unauthorized access problem will stop as long as lawbreakers can continue to make money from it.

The information in your credit files will not be safe until:

- You do a better job of protecting your personal and financial information.
- Credit bureaus improve their security systems.

- Tougher laws are passed to help secure your information and those who violate privacy laws are punished more severely.

Federal Privacy Laws

When the Constitution was written, the word privacy was not specifically mentioned, because this country's Founding Fathers believed that safeguards against physical searches and seizures adequately protected a citizen's privacy. Today, however, technology can search and seize some of the most personal details of your life without your knowledge. As a result, many of the federal privacy laws that are supposed to protect your privacy, including the FCRA, are inadequate. Many of them are outdated, while others are full of exemptions and loopholes that make the laws easy to circumvent.

In addition to the FCRA, some of the most important federal privacy laws are the Gramm-Leach-Biley Financial Modern-

WARNING

Many consumers and privacy organizations are alarmed about further erosions to consumer privacy as a result of the passage of the federal Patriot Act, which is part of this country's antiterrorism effort. Among other things, it gives the FBI and the CIA more power to wiretap and monitor residents and public gatherings and lets them come into your home without your permission or knowledge to search. Also, librarians and county clerks can be jailed for failing to disclose what you read or to turn over public records.

ization Act which was passed in 1999, the Privacy Act, the Right to Financial Privacy Act, the Video Privacy Protection Act, and the Computer Matching and Privacy Protection Act.

The Financial Modernization Act

The Financial Modernization Act, also known as the Gramm-Leach-Biley Act, was passed in 1999 to give banks, insurance companies, and brokerage firms the right to operate as single companies or "financial supermarkets." To help protect the highly sensitive information that these companies may have on you, the law gives you some control over what they can and cannot do with their information. Specifically, it says that financial institutions can share your personal information with the companies that they are affiliated with—a bank card company, an insurance company, or a brokerage firm, for example—as well as with companies with whom they have joint marketing agreements—direct mail marketers and telemarketers, for example. There is nothing that you can do to prevent this sharing.

Financial institutions *cannot* share your information with any other companies, assuming you tell them that you don't want them to share your information by formally opting out. Finan-

---

HOT TIP

When you receive information about your rights under the Financial Services Modernization Act, you will also be notified of your right to opt out of having the company share information related to your creditworthiness with its affiliated companies. You have this right under the FCRA.

cial institutions must offer you the opportunity to opt out each year. However, there is an exception to this requirement. A financial institution can share your information with another business, if that sharing is something it regularly does as a normal part of doing business. For example, it may have to share your information to get your checks printed or to produce your monthly bank statements.

Here is how the opt-out provision under the Financial Services Modernization works. Each year, the financial institutions (such as banks, bank card companies, and brokerage firms) with which you do business must provide you with printed information explaining the information they collect on their customers, what they do to keep that information safe, and the kinds of businesses to which they sell or give their information. They must also tell you how you can opt out of this information sharing.

Although this new law is a step forward, it has some serious weaknesses. For example, it does not do the following:

- *Establish a set format that financial institutions must use when they provide you with information regarding your opt-out rights under the law.* As a result, you may overlook the opt-out information when it is sent to you, especially if it is included with all of the notices and marketing offers that typically come with account billing statements, statements of accounts, and the like. If you don't see the information and, therefore, don't opt out, the financial institutions you deal with can do whatever they want with your personal and financial information.

- *Establish a specific method for opting out.* Each financial institution is free to establish its own process and requirements. Depending on the financial institution, therefore, you may have to opt out by calling a toll-free number, by completing and mailing back a printed form, or by going online. Furthermore, if you do not follow the exact procedure required by a financial institution, you will not be opted out.

- *Mandate a specific time of year during which financial institutions must provide you with opt-out information.* In other words, the opt-out information could arrive at any time within the 12-month period. Therefore, unless you know when to expect the opt-out information, you will have to make a point of going through every enclosure you receive with your account billing statements, account statements, and so on.

The Privacy Act of 1974

The Privacy Act of 1974 applies to federal agencies. It prohibits them from obtaining information for one purpose and then sharing it for another. However, because the information can be shared for "routine use," the law is virtually useless in terms of protecting your privacy. Any use can be defined as "routine."

The law also requires all local, state, and national government agencies that request your Social Security number to provide you with information that explains whether you must provide it, what will happen if you don't, and how the agencies will use it.

The Right to Financial Privacy Act

The Right to Financial Privacy Act governs the access of federal agencies to your bank records, but it includes exemptions for the FBI and U.S. attorneys and does not apply to private employers or to local and state governments. Because new exceptions seem to be added to this law on a regular basis, its ability to protect your financial privacy is being whittled away, little by little.

The Video Privacy Protection Act

The Video Privacy Protection Act forbids retailers from providing a list of the videos you rent to other businesses and individuals, unless you approve the release of the information or unless a court orders it. This law applies to video rental lists that are provided for free and to those that are sold.

The Computer Matching and Privacy Protection Act

The Computer Matching and Privacy Protection Act regulates the federal government's use of computer-matching techniques that compare data in one computer file to data in another to determine your eligibility for federal benefits. The law also limits the federal government's use of matching techniques to help it collect any money you may owe to the government. However, the law does not apply to many kinds of matches, including those done for law enforcement and tax collection purposes.

Privacy in the Credit Industry

As you have already learned from earlier chapters in this book, the larger credit bureaus market a variety of products and services in addition to producing and selling credit reports. Critics argue that these other products and services have taken credit bureaus beyond their original mission of helping creditors make credit-granting decisions, helping employers make hiring decisions, aiding insurers in their decisions regarding coverage, and helping landlords rent to creditworthy tenants. Although some of the FCRA amendments that were adopted in 1996 have helped protect the privacy of consumers by limiting what credit bureaus can do with the information in their databases, other amendments have made your information less private.

Data Mining and Warehousing

Data mining occurs when retailers, credit card issuers, and other creditors search and analyze their own databases and other sources of consumer information, including credit bureau records, to maximize the amount of information they have on current and potential customers. In doing this, their goals are, among other things, to improve their credit-granting decisions and to formulate better debt collection strategies. The information they mine is often described as being stored in data warehouses. All of the national credit bureaus have purchased, merged with, or formed strategic alliances with data mining/warehouse companies.

How Information Brokers Use Information

Some information brokers operate as legitimate, law-abiding businesses, but others break the law by selling consumer information to direct marketers, including telemarketers. Such sales are a violation of the FCRA. Some information brokers also develop, maintain, and market extensive demographic databases for targeted marketing. Although these databases are separate from those that credit bureaus, including the big three, maintain for credit-granting purposes, information brokers may enhance their databases with information they obtain from credit bureaus and from other sources, including phone books, the Census Bureau, subscription lists, real estate and insurance records, and consumer product warranty information. As a result, information brokers can create very precise and detailed profiles of consumers' spending habits, lifestyles, hobbies, work, friends, family, and other information. That information can be extremely valuable to direct marketers.

Special Products and Services

Most of the privacy-related criticism that has been directed at credit bureaus focuses on three of their products and services: prescreening, data enhancement, and targeted marketing databases.

Prescreening

Prescreening is a technique by which a credit bureau uses its consumer information to create a list of consumers who are qualified to receive a preapproved offer of credit or insurance. According to the FCRA, prescreening is legal so long as all of the individuals on the prescreened list receive a "firm offer" of credit or insurance.

Credit bureaus may create a prescreened list in one of two ways. One way is for a creditor or insurance company to supply a credit bureau with a set of characteristics that describe the market that the business wants to target to sell a particular product or service. For example, a national bank card company may want to offer a preapproved card to consumers who make more than $100,000 a year, have flawless credit records, and who have several unused lines of credit of $5,000 or more. The credit bureau that creates the list for the bank card company will compare those characteristics to the characteristics of the consumers in its database and generate a list of consumers who fit the bill. The bank card company will market its offer to the names on the list.

The other way that prescreened lists are created is when a creditor or insurance company provides a credit bureau with a list of consumers and a set of criteria that define the specific type of individual it wants to target. The business may have obtained its list from a list broker or from the credit bureau itself. The credit bureau compares the information in its database with the set of criteria to identify which of the consumers in its database should receive an offer of credit or insurance.

HOT TIP

If you see the letters *prm* or the word *promotional* in the inquiries section of your credit report, then your credit file was prescreened for an offer.

Critics object to prescreening because it is done without your knowledge or permission. They also worry that sophisticated technologies allow the companies that purchase prescreened lists to learn very specific information about a consumer's financial life, even though they never actually see the information in the consumer's credit file. Critics also allege that prescreening violates the intent of the FCRA, because prescreening has nothing to do with *your* solicitation of credit but relates instead to the efforts of a *business* to market its products or services to you. On the other hand, supporters of prescreening argue that the process actually benefits consumers by increasing the likelihood that the solicitations they receive in the mail will be for products and services in which they are interested and by reducing the number of unwanted solicitations. Many consumers would probably not agree with these arguments, however.

You have the right to opt out of receiving prescreened offers. In fact, amendments to the FCRA require the three national credit bureaus to maintain a toll-free phone number for opting out. If you call the number, the credit bureaus must, within five business days, remove your name from their lists of consumers whose information can be prescreened, and it must stay removed

WARNING

If you try to take advantage of a prescreened offer, you may be turned down for it, because amendments to the FCRA allow creditors and insurance companies to establish additional criteria besides the ones they give to the credit bureau that does their prescreening. You may not meet those other criteria even though you are on the prescreened list.

> ### H O T   T I P
>
> The federal government has established a national do-not-call registry. Go to <www.donotcall.gov> to register your phone number. Your registration will be effective for five years.

for five years. You can also extend the opt-out term for an additional five years. The number to call is 888-567-8688. However, you won't see an immediate reduction in prescreened offers after you call the number. It may take a couple months before that happens.

You can further eliminate the number of direct mail solicitations and telemarketing calls you receive, as well as the amount of spam in your e-mail inbox, by opting out with the Direct Marketing Association (DMA). The DMA is a national organization of direct marketers, including telemarketers. Figure 9.1 tells you how to opt out through the DMA.

> ### H O T   T I P
>
> FACTA now gives you the right to opt out of receiving prescreened offers from affiliated companies. These businesses are required to notify consumers that they may use their personal information for marketing purposes and provide the choice to opt out.

FIGURE 9.1
Opting Out through the DMA

After your have called the credit reporting industry's opt-out toll-free number, get in touch with the DMA to further reduce the number of solicitations you receive via mail as well as by phone and e-mail. Once you opt out, you will remain on the DMA's mail and telemarketing opt-out lists for five years, and you will stay on its e-mail opt-out list for two years. For more information on opting out, go to the DMA's consumer assistance Web site at <www.dmaconsumers.org/consumerassistance>.

Direct Marketing Association
Mail Preference Service, P.O. Box 9008
Farmington, NY 11735

Direct Marketing Association
Telephone Preference Service, P.O. Box 9014
Farmington, NY 11735

Direct Marketing Association
E-Mail Preference Service
<www.dmaconsumers.org/consumers/optoutform_emps.shtml>

Also, your state may have established its own opt-out program. Contact the consumer protection office of your state's attorney general to find out. Take advantage of all opt-out opportunities.

Although opting out won't mean a complete end to direct marketing efforts, it will reduce their volume. However, it probably won't reduce the number of solicitations you receive from charities, religious organizations, professional and alumni associations, political candidates, or local merchants.

Beyond the National Credit Bureaus

It used to be that most privacy-related criticism was directed at the credit reporting industry because of the sheer volume of

> # WARNING
>
> The further your information travels from the credit bureau that originally collected it, the more opportunities there are for that information to be used inappropriately and for unauthorized persons to acquire it.

information in their databases, the many ways that credit bureaus use the information, and the fact that so many consumers are affected by credit bureaus. However, by focusing just on credit bureaus, you ignore other threats to your privacy.

For example, information brokers are also a threat to your privacy. As this chapter has already explained, information brokers may purchase consumer credit information from the three national credit bureaus and then sell it and other database information to third-party users. In fact, disreputable information brokers may sell their information to anyone willing to buy it—for the right amount of money. These companies are able to get away with what they do, because they tend to be less visible than the three national credit bureaus. Thus, their activities do not receive as much attention and scrutiny by the public, watch dog groups, the FTC, and policy makers. Also, unscrupulous information brokers understand the weaknesses in the FCRA and capitalize on them.

Data Enhancement

Data enhancement is another way that your privacy can be violated. Data enhancement occurs when a company improves the quality and effectiveness of its database by adding selected information from other databases, including Census data, consumer surveys, product registration/warranty cards, and public records. A company may do this to learn more about its customers in order to sell them more products or services or to create lists that it can sell to other companies and organizations.

Critics of data enhancement argue that the practice helps companies create marketing lists that are as effective as prescreened lists but have broader applications. They also object to it, because once a consumer's personal information is in another company's database, the consumer has little control over how the information will be used. Also, like prescreening, data enhancement is done without your knowledge or permission.

Government and Privacy

The federal government also poses a threat to your privacy, because it collects and stores large volumes of information about consumers. In fact, even before it began its antiterrorism efforts in response to September 11, the federal government was the nation's largest data gatherer. For example, numerous federal agencies and departments maintain extensive databases on countless consumers—the FBI, the IRS, the Census Bureau, and the Drug Enforcement Administration (DEA), for example. Furthermore, despite the Federal Privacy Act, many federal agencies and departments link up their databases to search for consumer matches. Frequently, these agencies also match the information in their databases with information they purchased from private companies. In fact, the IRS uses this technique to locate tax nonfilers.

Profiling

Some government agencies use a technique called profiling to identify people who may be at risk for a particular kind of illegal behavior. Profiling involves identifying characteristics that are believed to be common to a group such as terrorists, tax evaders, drug smugglers, or welfare cheaters. The government agency doing the profiling compares those characteristics to the characteristics of individuals within the population at large or within a specific group to identify individuals who fit the profile.

Although no one can fault the IRS for wanting to crack down on tax evaders or the DEA for trying to reduce drug smuggling, privacy advocates object to profiling. They are concerned about the accuracy of profiling and worry because innocent people have been detained, even prosecuted, for no reason other than that they fit a particular profile. They also worry because there are few restrictions on profiling, leaving the practice open to potential abuse, and because nothing stops government agencies from expanding the use of profiling.

The Privacy of Your Medical Information

Your financial information is not the only thing that may not be private these days. Your medical information may be at risk, too, because hospitals, HMOs, doctors' offices, self-insured corporations, and insurance companies all have information about you in their databases. Some of their information may be highly sensitive—the fact that you are being treated for a mental health problem like depression, that you were treated for a sexually transmitted disease, that you had breast cancer, and so on. Ironically, although a court order is needed for the release of your video rental records, someone can relatively easily learn what is in your medical files, especially now that so much of that information is shared electronically between huge managed care organizations and medical providers.

The Medical Privacy Rule

The Health Insurance Portability and Accountability Act (HIPA) was enacted in 1996. Among other things, this law included a provision requiring either that Congress pass a medical privacy law governing the electronic transmission of patients' medical information by August 21, 1999, or that the Secretary of the U.S. Department of Health and Human Services (DHHS) draft a Rule governing that issue. Congress missed its chance, so privacy became the responsibility of the DHHS. The Clinton administration enacted an initial Medical Privacy Rule, which the Bush administration subsequently modified.

The current Medical Privacy Rule applies to all medical consumers. Unfortunately, although the original purpose of the Rule when HIPA was passed was to give health care consumers greater control over their medical records, the Rule does just the opposite. It makes it okay for doctors (even doctors who are not treating you), hospitals, insurers, public health agencies, data processing firms, law enforcement officials, some researchers, and the federal government to share your medical records electronically, including your genetic information, without your consent, when the information is needed to treat you, to process your claims, to reimburse you or a medical provider, and for "healthcare operations," a term so broad that it can be applied to just about any use. In essence, with adoption of the Medical Privacy Rule, you have lost control of your health and medical information.

Here are some of the key provisions of the Medical Privacy Rule.

- Generally, you are entitled to review your own medical records, including your doctor's notes, X rays, and lab results. You can also obtain copies of your medical records, although you may have to pay for them, and you are entitled to ask that any errors in those records be corrected. If you ask for access to your records, you should receive them within 30 days.
- Covered health plans, doctors, and other health care providers must tell you in writing how they may use your medical information and what your rights are under the Rule. You have no right to try to limit or control the uses.
- Covered health care plans, doctors, and other health care providers can share your medical information among themselves for purposes related to your medical care and treatment. However, they cannot share your information for purposes not related to health care.
- You have the right to ask a covered health plan, doctor, or other health care provider to limit the use of your

medical information *beyond* what is described in their written notices. However, they are not legally obligated to comply with your request.

- Covered health care plans, doctors, and other health care providers must get your written permission before they share your medical information with a life insurance company, bank, marketing firm, or some other business that is not related to your health care.

- Pharmacies, covered health plans, and other covered businesses must get your permission before they disclose information about you for marketing purposes.

- Covered health plans, doctors, pharmacies, and other covered businesses must establish policies and procedures to protect your medical privacy. However, the Rule does not establish any requirements regarding these policies and procedures. Also, they must describe these policies and procedures to you in writing.

- You have the right to file a formal complaint against a covered health plan, health care provider, or other covered business for wrongfully disclosing medical information about you. You must file your written complaint within 180 days of the disclosure. You can learn more

WARNING

Presently, state laws require that you give your consent before your medical information can be shared with others. However, it is expected that the insurance and medical industries will exercise their clout in the near future to ensure that the federal Rule will preempt state medical privacy laws.

about how to file a complaint by calling 866-627-7748 or by going to <www.hhs.gov/ocr/hipaa>.

- You have the right to sue a covered business for violating your rights under the Rule. The Rule provides for civil penalties of up to $100 per violation and up to $25,000 a year for each requirement or prohibition that is violated. There are also penalties for certain kinds of acts, ranging up to $50,000 and one year in prison for some offenses; up to $100,000 and as many as five years in prison for offenses committed under "false pretenses"; and up to $250,000 and up to 10 years in prison if the offense involves an intent to sell, transfer, or use protected medical information for commercial advantage, personal gain, or malicious harm.

The Medical Information Bureau

Although the Medical Information Bureau (MIB) does not maintain medical information on most American consumers, it may have a file on you. The MIB is a membership organization of about 600 life insurance companies. The MIB was established in 1902 by the medical directors of some insurance companies to

---

HOT TIP

Before an MIB member can request a copy of your MIB report in connection with your application for life, health, or disability insurance, it must get your written permission to do so, and it must provide you with information explaining how you can correct any problems in your MIB record.

reduce the number of fraudulent claims. Although fraud detection continues to be one of its functions, the organization now has a broader potential impact on consumers. For example, the information in a consumer's MIB file can affect his or her ability to obtain health, life, or disability insurance and to be reimbursed for a claim. It may also affect a consumer's employment opportunities if an insurer shares information from his or her MIB file with the consumer's current or potential future employer.

If you have medical insurance and require medical care, you or your doctor will file a claim with your insurance carrier/ HMO/PPO to get reimbursed. The claim information may be shared with the MIB if the insurance company/HMO/PPO is a member of that organization. Then, when another MIB member requests your file, the information related to that claim will be in it. Therefore, the information you thought you were telling your doctor in the strictest of confidence may eventually become part of a vast national medical information network if you subsequently apply for new insurance or increased coverage. According to the MIB, MIB members provide it with information about a consumer if, "an applicant has a condition significant to health or longevity." This information could include your height and weight, blood pressure, EKG readings, and X-ray results. However, some nonmedical information may also be reported to the MIB, including information about your driving record if you have a bad record, or the fact that you participate in a hazardous sport—you sky dive or race motorcycles, for example.

The FCRA governs the MIB's activities and, in fact, the FTC has begun holding it and other similar companies to many of the same standards that apply to credit reporting agencies. For example, the FTC has ruled that if an insurance company denies you health, life, or disability coverage or increases the cost of the insurance you already have because of information it obtained from the MIB or from a similar company, the insurer must give you the name and contact information of the company that supplied the information.

You have a right to a free copy of your MIB file if you request it within 30 days of being denied the insurance you want or experiencing some other adverse action, as long as the organization that took the adverse action indicates in its notice that the MIB was a source of information about you. Be sure to send a copy of this notice with your request for a free report.

If you have not been denied life, health, or disability insurance but you want to know whether the MIB has a file on you and what's in your file, you can purchase your MIB report for $9.00. Whether you are entitled to a free report or not, you have several options for ordering it.

- Write to the Medical Information Bureau, Inc., PO Box 105, Essex Station, Boston, MA 02112.
- Call the MIB at 617-426-3660.
- Go online to <www.mib.com>.

Employers and Privacy

As you have already learned from this book, when you apply for a new job or for a promotion with your current employer, the employer may review your credit record information as part of its decision-making process. Your employer may also review that information to make other employment-related decisions—whether to demote you, give you a raise, fire you, and so on. However, critics have questioned the predictive value of credit record information when it comes to personnel decisions. They are also concerned that misinformation in your credit record could cost you an important employment opportunity, despite your qualifications.

To help protect consumers, the FCRA now requires that employers obtain the written permission of an employee or prospective employee before they review his or her credit history. The law also states that, before an employer can take an adverse action against an employee or prospective employee due in whole or in part to information in that person's credit file, the employer must provide him or her with a copy of the credit file it reviewed together with information about his or her right to dispute any errors. The employer must also give the individual the name and address of the credit bureau that provided it with the negative information.

Private Databases for Employers

In addition to reviewing your credit report information before making an employment decision, some employers may review information in other databases that are designed to provide very specific kinds of information. For example, some databases tell employers whether someone has filed a lot of claims for on-the-job injuries, together with information about the claims and about any lawsuits that may have resulted. Other databases tell employers whether a particular employee or prospective employee has ever been arrested, even if the arrest did not result in a conviction. Still others indicate whether a particular employee or prospective employee is a "trouble maker."

What is particularly alarming about these databases is that there is no way for you to know if the information they may contain on you is accurate, because the FCRA doesn't apply to them. Therefore, you have no legal right to review the information in these databases and no right to have inaccurate information corrected or deleted. Yet you could miss out on an important job opportunity because of the information in a private database.

Psychological Testing

Some employers use psychological testing to help screen out "problem" job applicants. The testing can put applicants in a precarious position—if they don't agree to the testing, they won't get the job; but if they take the test and answer honestly, they may reveal highly personal information about themselves and not get the job. Furthermore, if they are hired and sensitive personal information about them is retained in their employer's database, they will have no way of knowing who might see that information, whether it will be used against them, or where it might end up.

Online Technology

The Internet has opened up seemingly limitless opportunities for your privacy to be invaded. For example, every move you make and every site you visit can be monitored by Web site operators, and efforts to reduce the kind and amount of spam you receive over the Internet have not been particularly effective. Web site operators can develop highly detailed portraits of your interests and preferences to customize their products and services and to make sure that their marketing approach has special appeal to you. Furthermore, when you provide information about yourself to a Web site, the information may get sold to other companies without your knowledge or, it goes without saying, your permission. Also, online entrepreneurs can purchase your e-mail address from online companies that are in the business of compiling and selling such information.

CHAPTER 10

How to Protect Yourself from the Crime of Identity Theft

My neighbor, Susan M., was close to tears the afternoon she stopped by my home. When I asked her what was wrong, she told me that she had been turned down for a promotion, which would have meant a considerable increase in her salary, because of information in her credit record. Susan told me that when she reviewed the credit report her employer had looked at, she discovered that it included several accounts with negative histories and very high balances. However, she had not opened those accounts or run up those balances. Susan asked me if I could explain how that information could have ended up in her credit record and what she could do to get it out of there. She was worried because she had always had a good credit history, but now it appeared to be ruined.

I told Susan that she was probably the victim of identity theft—that someone may have stolen her personal and financial information and used it to open credit accounts in her name, using her credit history. I also explained that identity theft has become a major threat to consumers. In fact, according to the U.S. Justice Department, as many as 700,000 consumers may be the victims of identity theft each year. In 2003, the Federal Trade Commission (FTC) reported that identity theft complaints represented 43 percent of all the consumer complaints it had received during the previous year, and that the problem was at the top of its most common consumer frauds list for the third year in a row. I told Susan to come by my office the next day so we could discuss what she should do about the theft of her identity and how to avoid becoming a victim of identity theft again. I also explained that because of FACTA, Susan now had new tools for protecting herself against identity theft, and minimizing the impact of that crime on her life.

This chapter provides you with much of the same information and advice that I provided to Susan. It explains what identity theft is and how it is accomplished and tells you how to avoid becoming a victim. It also tells you exactly what to do if you are victimized, including how to use the identity-theft FACTA provisions.

What Is Identity Theft?

Identity theft is a federal crime under the Identity Theft and Assumption Deterrence Act. It occurs when someone steals

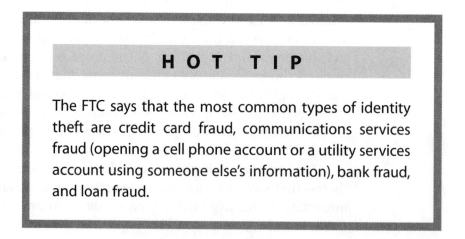

HOT TIP

The FTC says that the most common types of identity theft are credit card fraud, communications services fraud (opening a cell phone account or a utility services account using someone else's information), bank fraud, and loan fraud.

your personal and/or financial information to use your credit accounts, tap your bank accounts, get new credit in your name, file fraudulent tax returns, get a cell phone in your name, access your insurance benefits, and so on. Identity thieves may carry out their crimes by stealing your Social Security number, name, credit card number, bank account number, driver's license number, the serial number for your cell phone, your ATM PIN, and anything else that could be used by itself or in combination with other information to identify you.

Many states have their own identity theft laws. At the time this book was written, these states were:

Alabama	Louisiana	Ohio
Alaska	Maine	Oklahoma
Arizona	Maryland	Oregon
Arkansas	Massachusetts	Pennsylvania
California	Michigan	Rhode Island
Connecticut	Minnesota	South Carolina
Delaware	Missouri	South Dakota
Florida	Montana	Tennessee
Georgia	Nebraska	Texas
Hawaii	Nevada	Utah
Idaho	New Hampshire	Virginia
Illinois	New Jersey	Washington
Indiana	New Mexico	West Virginia
Iowa	New York	Wisconsin
Kansas	North Carolina	Wyoming
Kentucky	North Dakota	

If you live in one of these states, get in touch with the consumer protection office of your state attorney general's office. If your state is not among those listed here, it may have passed a law since this book was written, or identity theft may be prohibited under another law in your state. Again, call your state attorney general's office to find out.

When someone steals your personal and financial information, your life may become a living hell, especially if you don't realize what has happened right away and the identity thief has

---

WARNING

The CCRRA and FACTA pre-empt some provisions of current and future state identity theft laws.

---

time to seriously damage your finances. You may discover that something is amiss when you check the balance in your bank account or review your bank card billing statement. However, you may not find out what has happened until debt collectors begin hounding you about unpaid debts that you know nothing about, you are billed for a service you never contracted for, your check is refused by a retail store, or you review your credit record like Susan M. did.

Identity thieves may obtain your personal and financial information in a variety of ways. For example, they may:

- Steal your wallet, purse, or handheld computer
- Go through the mail in your mailbox

WARNING

According to a recent national survey conducted by Garntner, Inc. in Stamford, Connecticut, 53 percent of reported identity theft cases involve a relative, friend, or coworker stealing the identification of someone they know. Thirty-four percent involve a stranger stealing someone's wallet, and 13 percent involve the theft of someone's mail.

- Search your trash and recycling for papers with an account number or your Social Security number
- Eavesdrop on your phone conversations when you are talking on a cell phone or at a pay phone.
- Remove information from your personnel file at your place of employment
- Hack into your computer
- Buy your information over the Internet
- Copy your account number from one of your credit card receipts, checks, credit applications, and so on
- Trick you into sharing your personal and financial information with them via e-mail or during a conversation

The longer it takes for you to discover that your identity has been stolen, the tougher it will probably be to resolve the problem. In fact, getting your identity back could take months

---

HOT TIP

You may have a strong case against a credit bureau and/or a creditor if your credit record was damaged because an identity thief obtained new credit in your name and did not pay that debt. If you inform the credit bureau of the crime and ask it to stop reporting information about the fraudulent debt, yet it continues to do so, consult with a consumer law attorney. Do the same if you inform the creditor associated with a fraudulent account that you are the victim of identity theft and the creditor continues to report information about that account to the credit bureau. Chapter 4 provides resources for finding a consumer law attorney who can help you.

> ### W A R N I N G
>
> Some identity thieves work for banks, credit unions, brokerage firms, insurance companies, restaurants, retail outlets, and the like. Their positions make it easy for them to gain access to the information of customers or coworkers.

and even years. Therefore, it is important to be proactive when it comes to identity theft by knowing how to protect yourself. It is also important that you know what to do right away if you are victimized.

How to Protect Yourself from Identity Theft

As you learned in the previous chapter, in today's information-oriented, high-tech world, protecting the privacy of your personal and financial information can be a challenge, despite laws

> ### W A R N I N G
>
> Your Social Security number can be a gold mine for an identity thief because that number alone may let the criminal apply for credit cards in your name, open bank accounts, get a loan, rent a place to live, benefit from your insurance, and so on.

that have been passed to help you do that. Truth is, however, those laws will never be able to protect your information completely, because there will always be companies and individuals who will figure out how to get around them. Ultimately, it is up to you to protect your personal and financial information. Therefore, the following list highlights actions you can take to keep your information safe. Many of these actions will also alert you to the fact that your identity has been stolen.

- Monitor the information in your credit records by ordering a copy of them from each of the three national credit bureaus every six months. Another way to monitor that information is to subscribe to the credit monitoring services of Equifax, Experian, and TransUnion. If you do, they will notify you via e-mail whenever anyone applies for credit in your name, and you will have unlimited access to your credit report. At the time this book was written, the cost of this service ranged from $45 to $80 a year per credit bureau.
- Follow the opt-out advice in Chapter 9.
- Use cash rather than credit to pay for things whenever possible. When you pay with cash, you won't leave behind a receipt that shows your account number and your signature. Two added benefits of paying with cash are that the details of your transaction are less likely to end up in a business's database and you will be less apt to develop credit problems.
- Never leave an intact credit card receipt carbon behind. Take it with you.
- Don't carry your Social Security card in your wallet or purse, and don't carry every credit card and ID you have. Keep only what you need in your purse or wallet.
- Sign your credit cards as soon as they arrive.
- If you apply for a new credit card and it does not arrive within a reasonable period of time, call the card issuer. It is possible that an identity thief stole the new card from your mailbox. Do the same thing if you do not receive a replacement card for a credit card you already have.

- Protect your handheld computer.
- Carefully review your credit card billing statements each month for any charges you don't understand or didn't make.
- Purchase a home shredder and shred anything with your name and address, account number, PIN number, Social Security number, and the like on it, including preapproved offers for credit, rather than throwing the information away. You can purchase a good home shredder for as little as $30.
- Never give your ATM or debit card PIN to anyone, and don't write the number on your card or keep it with your card.
- Shield your PIN from others when you use your ATM or debit card.
- Don't leave your ATM receipts where strangers can pick them up, and never toss them in the trash without ripping them up first. Better yet, take them home and shred them.
- Don't share your personal information just because someone asks for it. Be sure that you know with whom you are dealing and that they really need the information. For example, some businesses ask you about yourself and your finances just to be able to market to you later.
- When you write a check to pay for a credit card bill, don't write your account number on your check. Just write the last four digits of the account.
- Don't have your Social Security number or driver's license number printed on your checks.
- Keep your driver's license number to yourself as much as possible. In some states, this number is the same as your Social Security number.
- When you purchase something with a check or a credit card, don't write your Social Security number on the check or on the part of the credit receipt that the merchant will keep. No law requires that you provide your Social Security number when you purchase something with a credit card or a check. However, a merchant can

refuse to do business with you if you won't provide the number.

- Put your work number, not your home phone number, on your checks.

- Order new checks with your first initials and last name, rather than your full name. That way, an identity thief won't know how to sign your name.

- Don't write your telephone number or address on a merchant's credit slip or receipt. No law requires that you do. In fact, some states prohibit merchants from asking consumers to provide this information so that it can be recorded on their receipts or sales slips.

- Think twice before you respond to a telephone or written survey. Direct marketers and others may sell the information in your responses.

- Limit what information you provide when you complete a warranty card, product registration form, mail order form, and the like.

- Think twice before you respond to a mail or phone offer. If you do, your name, address, and telephone number will probably end up on at one least other direct marketing list.

- Don't share your Social Security number, credit card account numbers, or other personal information over the Internet unless you are sure that you are dealing with a secure site. A key or lock will appear on your computer screen if the site is secure; a broken key or lock will appear if it is not.

- Don't respond to any e-mails that seem suspicious or that come from strangers or organizations with which you are unfamiliar.

- Find out how your Internet service provider protects the consumer credit-related information in its database.

- Don't respond to junk e-mail. In addition to threatening your privacy, a lot of it is nothing more than consumer scams. Steer clear!

- If you subscribe to an online service, online newsletters, and so on, avoid obvious passwords such as your birth date, consecutive numbers, the last several digits in your Social Security number or mother's maiden name.

- Add passwords to your phone and utility accounts, credit card accounts, bank accounts, and so on.
- Take your outgoing mail to the post office rather than depositing it in your mail box. Some identity thieves steal mail to obtain information.
- If you are planning to leave town for a couple days, ask a trusted friend or neighbor to bring in your mail.
- Be careful what you say when you are in a public place and talking on the phone. An identity thief may overhear your conversation or use a special scanning device to eavesdrop if you are speaking on a cell phone.
- Store any personal information you keep at work in a locked drawer. If you are throwing away any mail or paperwork that includes your personal and/or financial information, tear it into small pieces first or shred it.
- Find out what your employer is doing to secure your personnel and payroll information. It could be a gold mine for an identity thief.

W A R N I N G

Many banks, credit card companies, and other financial institutions use Social Security numbers to identify and maintain information on their customers. In addition, many computerized data bases use Social Security numbers for identification purposes. Given the frequency with which Social Security numbers are used, it is easy for identity thieves to steal the numbers and use them to access a broad range of information.

> ### WARNING
>
> According to the Identity Theft Resource Center in San Diego, nine out of ten identity thefts involve the theft of payroll or employment files.

- Take advantage of all opt-out opportunities. The less your information is shared by companies and the fewer direct marketing and prescreened offers you receive, the fewer opportunities thieves will have to use that information to steal your identity.

Another Step to Take, Just in Case

Despite your efforts to protect your personal and financial information, your identity could still be stolen. For example, you could lose your purse, wallet, and/or handheld computer, and the person who finds the missing item(s) could steal your credit cards, IDs, checkbook, ATM card, and so on. Therefore,

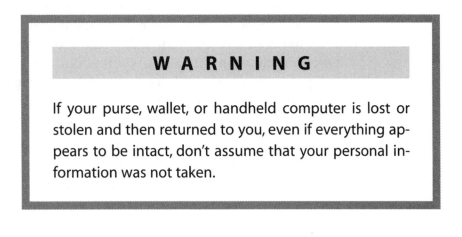

> ### WARNING
>
> If your purse, wallet, or handheld computer is lost or stolen and then returned to you, even if everything appears to be intact, don't assume that your personal information was not taken.

create a record of all your credit cards, bank accounts, ATM and debit cards, and brokerage accounts, including the name of each business you have an account with, contact information for each business, and all applicable account numbers. The list should also include similar information for any other cards and IDs that you regularly carry. Store this list in a safe place but not in your purse, wallet, or handheld computer and keep it up-to-date. The list will be invaluable if your identity is stolen or if your purse, wallet, or handheld computer is lost or stolen.

What to Do If You Think You Are a Victim of Identity Theft

If you believe that an identity thief has victimized you or you believe that you may become a victim—your wallet was stolen or lost, for example—take the following steps right away. Remember, the sooner you act, the less damage the thief can do to your finances.

Contact the Three National Credit Bureaus

Each of the three national credit reporting agencies has a special fraud alert department that helps consumers with their identity theft problems. Therefore, if you believe that you have been the victim of identity theft or that you may become a victim, it is important that you contact these departments right away by calling their fraud alert hotlines so that you can get a fraud alert and a victim's statement added to each of your credit files. That way, whenever an authorized user reviews the information in one of those files, it will find out about your identity theft problem. Also, creditors will check with you before they open a new account in your name or change anything related to one of your existing accounts. The numbers to call are:

Equifax	800-525-6285
Experian	800-397-3742
TransUnion	800-680-7289

Presently, most fraud alerts last for 60 to 90 days. However, you can extend an alert for up to seven years. Put your request in writing.

You have a right to a free copy of your credit report from each of the credit bureaus you contact about the identity fraud, so be sure to ask for it if they don't send you your free copies automatically. Review each report for any new accounts that may have been opened fraudulently, for charges that you do not recognize, and for any other signs that an identity thief has been using your accounts. If you find signs of fraud, ask the credit bureau that is reporting the information for the names and addresses of the creditors associated with the accounts so that you can contact them. You should also request that the credit bureau remove from your record all inquiries related to the fraudulent accounts, as well as all of the fraudulent account information.

After you have gotten your credit record information correct, order a copy of your credit reports a month or two later so that you can confirm that the fraudulent information is not still being reported, and to ensure that no new problems related to the theft of your identity have cropped up.

FACTA Requires That a New One-Call Fraud Alert Process Replace Existing Fraud Alert Process

FACTA has added a variety of provisions to the FCRA related to identity theft. One of the provisions that will be most helpful to consumers is the establishment of a one-call fraud alert system, which should make it quicker and easier for you to get fraud alerts added to all three of your credit files. Once this system is in place, rather than having to contact the fraud alert department of all three credit bureaus, you will be able to contact just one credit reporting agency and it will be obligated to pass your identity theft alert information on to the other two credit bureaus. They in turn must add your alert to the credit files they maintain on you. In addition, all three of the national credit bureaus must report the alert whenever they provide your credit record information or your credit score to an authorized user. For details on the one-call fraud alert system once it is in place, go to the author's Web site <www.johnventura.com>. Information should also be available directly from the credit bureaus.

Under FACTA, once the first credit bureau has added a fraud alert to your credit file, it must notify you of your right to obtain upon your request one or more free copies of your credit report from each of the three credit bureaus during the year following the start of the alert. When you request your credit report from a credit bureau, it must provide it within three days of receiving your request, and it must also send a copy of an FTC-prepared summary of your rights as an identity theft victim.

Under FACTA There Are Three Different Types of Fraud Alerts

FACTA has established three different types of fraud alerts. These alerts will replace the current fraud alert.

1. *A standard alert.* This kind of alert is quick and easy to initiate, but will stay in your credit file for only 90 days.
2. *An active military duty alert.* This alert applies if you are in the military on active duty, or if you are reservist who has been called to active duty and been assigned to a location that is away from your usual military station of duty. If you meet this definition, you can request that an active duty alert rather than a standard fraud alert be added to your credit file. The alert will remain in your credit file for months rather than just days 90 days, and it entitles you to two free copies of your credit report, upon request, from each of the national credit bureaus during this time. Also, for two years after the date of your request, the credit bureaus must exclude your name from all prescreened lists for offers of credit or insurance they may prepare.
3. *An extended alert.* This type of alert will remain in your credit file for seven years. To add an extended alert to your credit files, you must provide the credit reporting agency you contact to report your identity theft problem with a copy of your identity theft report. Although FACTA

does not define what constitutes such a report, and requires the FTC to make that determination, the law states that at a minimum the report must state your allegations of identity theft, must be a copy of an official report that you filed with a state, local, or federal law enforcement agency, and must subject you to criminal penalties if the information in the report is false and inaccurate. Once the FTC has determined how to file an identity theft report, that information will be available at the author's Web site <www.johnventura.com>. Once you have added an extended fraud alert to your credit files, you will be entitled to receive two free credit reports from each of the three national credit bureaus over the following year. Also, for the next five years, the credit reporting agencies must exclude you from any prescreened lists they may generate. When you request a copy of your free report, the credit bureaus must provide it within three days.

Regardless of what type of fraud alert you request, the alert in your credit files must state that you do not authorize the establishment of new credit in your name, other than the extension of credit under an existing open-end credit account such as a credit card, nor do you authorize the issuance of an additional card or an increase in the credit limit on one of your existing accounts. In addition, when there is an alert in your credit file, a

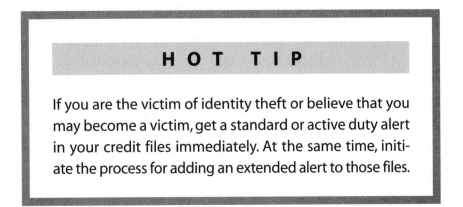

HOT TIP

If you are the victim of identity theft or believe that you may become a victim, get a standard or active duty alert in your credit files immediately. At the same time, initiate the process for adding an extended alert to those files.

creditor may not proceed with any of these types of credit transactions unless it uses "reasonable policies and procedures for forming a reasonable belief that the user knows the identity of the person making the request." In other words, the creditor has an obligation to make certain that the person it is dealing with is really you. Also, if the alert in your credit files includes your telephone number, prospective users of that information in those files must contact you using that number or "take reasonable steps" to verify that the person initiating the credit transaction is really you and not an identity thief.

For extra protection when your identity has been stolen or when you are concerned that you may become an identity theft victim, you can include a phone number in the alert when you file an extended fraud alert. Creditors must use that number to verify your identity when they have receive a request for new credit in your name, an increase in the credit limit on one of your existing accounts, and so on. Standard and active duty alerts do not give you the opportunity to add your phone number. Instead, users of your credit file information are expected to take "reasonable steps" to verify your identity when someone initiates a credit transaction using your name.

Other provisions of FACTA that relate to identity theft are described in Figure 10.1.

Get the Fraudulent Information Blocked Too

When you find fraudulent information in your credit file, FACTA also gives you the right to ask a credit bureau to block the information. That way, the information will no longer be included in your credit report or provided to creditors, insurance companies, or to anyone else who reviews your credit file. You should file a fraud alert and get the information blocked.

To get the information blocked, you must provide the credit bureau with the following:

- Proof of your identity

FIGURE 10.1
Other Identity Theft Protections Provided by FACTA

In addition to the identity theft related provisions that this chapter has discussed, FACTA also includes other provisions intended to help protect your identity. For example:

- FACTA requires businesses that produce point-of-sale electronically printed receipts as the result of a business transaction that you pay for with a credit or debit card to print just five digits of the card's account number and to omit the card's expiration date from the receipt. This requirement does not go into effect until December 4, 2006 for cash registers and other devices in use prior to January 1, 2005. For all other cash registers and other devices, the provision goes into effect on December 4, 2004.

- When you request a copy of your credit report, you are entitled to require that the credit bureau leave the last five digits of your Social Security number off the report.

- FACTA requires that users of consumer information that was derived from credit reports to dispose of that information according to regulations that the FTC, the federal banking agencies, and the National Credit Union Administration will develop. At the time this book was written, those regulations had not been developed. Once they are, they will be summarized at the author's Web site <www.johnventura.com>.

- If a business or another authorized user requests a copy of a consumer's credit report from a credit reporting agency and its request includes an address that is different from the one in the consumer's credit file, the credit reporting agency must notify the requester of this discrepancy. In turn, the requester must make sure that it knows the identity of the person to whom the credit report pertains. Also, if the requester establishes a continuing relationship with the consumer of that same credit reporting agency, it must help reconcile the discrepancy in addresses by providing the credit reporting agency with the address it was given by the consumer.

(continued)

FIGURE 10.1
Other Identity Theft Protections Provided by FACTA, continued

- The FTC, the federal banking agencies, and the National Credit Union Administration must work together to establish guidelines to help highlight possible instances of identity theft and to establish regulations related to polices and procedures for implementing those guidelines. The guidelines will apply to creditors and financial institutions.

- The FTC, the federal banking agencies, and the National Credit Union Administration must work together to develop regulations for issuers of credit cards to ensure that if a card issuer receives notification of an address change for an existing account, and during at least the first 30 days following receipt of the notice the issuer receives a request for an additional or replacement card for that same account, the issuer will use "reasonable policies and procedures" to notify the cardholder of the request at his or her former address before processing the request. The card issuer must also provide the cardholder with a means of promptly reporting any incorrect address changes.

- A copy of your identity theft report (As previously mentioned, the FTC will define what an identity theft report is, and when it does, the definition will appear on the author's Web site.)
- Identification of the information that you believe to be the result of identity theft
- A statement by you that the information you want blocked does not relate to any transaction you initiated

Once a credit bureau receives this information, it must add a block to your credit file within four business days and let the provider of the blocked information know that it has done so and why. Then the provider must take steps to avoid reeporting the blocked information to a credit bureau or to anyone else, either by deleting, modifying, or blocking that informa-

HOT TIP

Rather than waiting for a credit bureau to make contact with an information provider about information that you have asked to have blocked, you can trigger the provider's responsibilities regarding that information by contacting it directly and providing it with a copy of your identity theft report. However, you do not have the right to enforce the blocking provision if you initiate the block with the provider.

tion. Also, the provider is prohibited from selling or transferring any debt related to that information and sending the fraudulent debt to collections.

A credit bureau can refuse to comply with your request for an information block or can rescind a block if it determines that you erroneously requested the block, that the information was blocked in error, or that you misrepresented the facts in order to get a block. It can also deny your request for a block if it determines that you somehow benefited from the identity theft—you obtained goods, services, or money as a result of the identity theft, for example.

If a credit bureau refuses to put a block in place or rescinds an existing block, it must notify you in writing of its decision within five business days and must provide you with the name, address, and phone number "if reasonably available" of the provider of the information you asked to have blocked. In addition, the credit bureau must notify you of your right to add a written statement to your credit file regarding the information that it refused to block.

> ## H O T   T I P
>
> If a debt collector contacts you about a debt that you own and you tell the collector that you believe the debt is the result of identity theft, the debt collector must inform the creditor for whom it is trying to collect the debt of your allegation. It must also provide you with all the information you would be entitled to under the Fair Debt Collection Practices Act if you were in fact liable for the debt.

Get Copies of Any Applications the Identity Thief May Have Filled Out

In order to help you determine the identity of an identity thief who has victimized you and to prosecute that individual, FACTA gives you the right to request that a business that extended credit to, provided goods or services to, accepted payment from, or entered into some other commercial relationship with the individual who stole your identity provide you with free copies of any application the thief may have filled out, as well as copies of any business transaction the business may have conducted with that identity thief. However, the business does not have to provide you with Internet navigation data or similar information related to an application the identity thief filled out to any transaction between the business and the identity thief.

To obtain credit record and transaction records from a business, you must put your request in writing and mail it to whatever address the business may specify. Include with your request any relevant information related to the transaction that the business may need in order to meet its FACTA obligations. The information may include the date of the fraudulent application or business transaction, assuming you know it and can readily obtain this information, fraudulent account, or transaction numbers, and any other identifying information that you may have.

Before the business provides you with the information you request, it can require you to prove who you are by providing it with a government-issued ID card, the same type of identifying information the identity thief gave to the business, or the specific kind of identifying information the business typically requests from new applicants or for new transactions. The business can also ask you for proof that your identity was actually stolen. According to FACTA, acceptable proof includes:

- A copy of the police report related to your claim of identify theft
- A properly completed copy of the FTC's standard affidavit of identity theft (You can find this affidavit at the FTC's Web site <www.ftc.gov>.)
- An affidavit related to the theft of your identity that is acceptable to the business

If you cannot provide the business with the information it requests, if you provide it with the necessary information but

WARNING

If a business does not comply with this provision of FACTA, the law does not give you the right to enforce the provision—to sue, for example. Also, FACTA bars individual states from passing their own laws related to this particular matter. Therefore, the effectiveness of this particular FACTA provision depends on the willingness of businesses to comply with it.

the business is still not certain that you are who you claim to be, or if it believes that you have misrepresented information related to your request, the business can decline to provide you with the information you asked for.

Other Steps You Should Take If You Believe That You Are the Victim of Identity Theft

You should take other steps in addition to getting fraud alerts added to your credit files, getting the fraudulent information blocked, and requesting copies of any applications the identity thief may have filled out for a business that entered into a business relationship with the thief. You should also contact your local police and your creditors, and monitor your account billing statements, among other things. The rest of this chapter discusses these and other steps you should take and also tells you about additional resources that can help you when your identity has been stolen or when you believe it had been stolen.

Let the Police Know

Contact your local police department or the police department in the community where your personal or financial information was stolen, assuming you know. However, don't expect the police to launch an aggressive effort to determine who stole your identity, although you may get lucky and they may find the thief. In today's mobile, high-tech world, the criminal could live in another part of the country, far outside the jurisdiction of your local police department, or even in another part of the world. Plus, investigating allegations of identity theft is a fairly specialized process and may be beyond the skills of your local police. Expect that the police will prepare a report on the crime, because some of the financial companies with which you do business may want to see that report as proof that a crime was committed before they will help you. The report should list all of the items that you believe were stolen, even your health club membership card, insurance card, employee or student ID, as well as any cards with a PIN or pass code on them. Be sure to get a copy of the report and review it carefully. If you discover an error in the report or any missing information, ask the police department to revise the report so that it is complete and accurate.

If the police seem to be making your report a low priority, politely remind whomever you are dealing with that identity theft is a federal crime. If your state has its own identity theft law, mention that law, too.

Notify Creditors

Contact the fraud or security units for each of the creditors associated with any fraudulent accounts and charges you find in your credit files. Let them know that you are the victim of identity theft, that you did not make or authorize any of the charges, did not open the accounts, and want them closed right away. Also, ask that they stop reporting the fraudulent information to credit bureaus, and attach to your letter a copy of your identity theft report (as defined by the FTC) under FACTA. You should do this even if you have already asked that this information be blocked, as described in the previous section.

Then a couple of months later, review each of your credit records to ensure that the creditors complied with your requests. If they did not, make the requests again. You should also ask each creditor to what address you should send a letter that makes the same request, and then send your letter(s) immediately via certified mail, receipt requested. It is important to put your requests in writing, because if the identity thief has purchased things with your credit accounts and you let the applicable creditors know in writing, the Fair Credit Billing Act (FCBA) will protect you. This law says that if you contact a creditor about a charge on your account that you did not make and the creditor agrees that the charge is incorrect, you will not have to pay more than $50 of the unauthorized charges.

Ask each creditor to report to the credit bureau(s) it works with that the accounts are fraudulent and that they were closed at your request. In addition, ask the creditors to provide you with copies of all fraudulent transactions made in your name. You may need this information later.

Monitor the Billing Statements for Your Credit Accounts

Closely monitor all of your credit card billing statements for signs that the identity thief has used your cards. If that has happened, follow the advice in the previous section on how to exercise your FCBA rights. Also call the fraud unit for the credit card company(ies) to ask that your account be closed and that a new account be opened in your name. You should further request that the company report to the credit bureau(s) with which it works that the account was closed at your request. Review your credit reports a month or two later to make sure that the account was closed.

WARNING

Every creditor has its own process for handling a fraud charge. Therefore, when you contact a creditor about a fraudulent charge on one of your accounts, be sure that you understand your obligations as well as the creditor's for dealing with that charge and that you follow the creditor's instructions exactly. Otherwise, your complaint may not be handled in a timely manner. In addition, once a creditor has finished investigating your complaint, ask it for a letter stating that you are not responsible for the fraudulent charge(s).

If the identity thief has been writing checks on your account, notify the major check verification companies about the theft. They are:

Certigy	800-437-5120
CheckRite	800-766-2748
Chexsystems	800-428-9623
CrossCheck	800-843-0760
International Check Services	800-526-5380
SCAN	800-262-7771
Telecheck	800-710-9898

If Your Bank Accounts Have Been Tapped

Contact your bank, savings and loan, or credit union if the identity thief took money out of your account(s) without your permission. Do the same if your checks are lost or stolen. Put stop payments on any checks that were written on your account that you did not write. If you find out that the identity thief has opened new accounts in your name, get in touch with the fraud unit of the applicable financial institution to report the fraud and to ask that the account(s) be closed immediately. If your state has its own identity theft law, contact your state attorney general's office about how to report the identity theft.

HOT TIP

If a business refuses to accept your check after your identity has been stolen, ask it for the name of the check screening company it works with and then call that company to inform it of the identity theft.

H O T   T I P

When you contact a financial services company about a fraudulent account or fraudulent charge, you may be required to provide a copy of your police report, an identity theft report (as defined by the FTC), and/or a completed fraud affidavit. The FTC maintains a fraud affidavit at its Web site that you can fill out and that most businesses will accept. You can find the fraud affidavit online at <www.consumer.gov/idtheft/> or write to Identity Theft Clearinghouse, FTC, 600 Pennsylvania Avenue NW, Washington, DC 20580.

Call the Social Security Administration

If your Social Security card was stolen or if you believe that someone else is using your Social Security number, you should report your suspicion to the FTC using one of the three reporting options listed in the previous section.

If you think that someone is using your Social Security number to work, contact the Social Security Administration by calling its toll-free number, 800-772-1213. If you are not sure that someone is using your Social Security number to work, submit a *Request for Social Security Statement* (Form 7004) form. You can download a copy of this form at <www.socialsecurity.gov/online/ssa-7004.pdf>. You can also request the form by calling the administration's toll-free number or by visiting your local Social Security office. Your statement should arrive four to six weeks after you order it.

Your *Social Security Statement* lists the earnings that have been posted to your Social Security record during the years that you have been working, and it estimates the amount of Social Security benefits you and your family may be entitled to now and in the future. If you find any errors in your statement, call the Social Security Administration right away using its toll-free number.

Other Actions You May Need to Take

Depending on the nature of your identity theft problem, you may need to take some or all of the following actions:

- Cancel your ATM card and/or debit card if they have been lost, stolen, or used without your permission.
- Ask your insurance companies to issue you new policy numbers if you have reason to believe that a stranger is using your insurance or if your Social Security number was stolen and it is also used as your insurance ID number.
- Cancel your retail charge cards, long distance calling cards, video store cards, and so on, and ask for replacement cards if they are lost or stolen, or if you know that the card numbers are being used without your permission.
- If your driver's license has been stolen, contact your state motor vehicle department and arrange for a new license with a different number. Also, ask the department to add a lost or stolen driver's license warning to your file.
- If your passport is stolen, contact the U.S. State Department's Passport Office. You can do that online by going to <travel.state.gov/passport_services.html> or by calling 202-955-0292. You can also write to the U.S. Department of State, Passport Services, Consular Lost/Stolen Passport Section, 1111 19th Street, NW, #500, Washington, DC 20036.
- If your mail is stolen from your mailbox, call your local Postal Inspector. You can get that number by calling 800-275-8777 or by going to <www.usps.gov/webites/depart/inspect>.
- Call your long distance carrier and/or cell phone company if your phone bills reflect charges that neither you

FIGURE 10.2
Identity Theft Resources You Should Know About

There are a growing number of resources available to help consumers avoid becoming victims of identity theft and to deal with the problem if they are victimized. Here are some of the organizations that can help you and the URLs for their Web sites:

- The Department of Justice, <www.usdoj.gov>

- The Federal Bureau of Investigation, <www.fbi.gov>

- The Federal Trade Commission, <www.ftc.gov> and <www.consumer.gov/idtheft>

- Future Crime, <www.futurecrime.com>

- Identity Theft Resource Center, <www.idtheftcenter.org>

- IRS, <www.trea.gov/irs/ci>

- Privacy Rights Clearinghouse, <www.privacyrights.org>

- U.S. Public Interest Research Group (PIRG), <www.pirg.org>

- National Fraud Organization, <www.fraud.org>

- National Center for Victims of Crime, <www.ncvc.org>

- National White Collar Crime Center, <www.iir.com/nwccc>

- National Criminal Justice Reference Service, <www.cnjrs.org>

- Securities and Exchange Commission, <www.sec.gov>

- Social Security Administration, <www.ssa.gov>

- U.S. Bankruptcy Trustee, <www.usdoj.gov.ust>

- U.S. Postal Service, <www.usps.gov/websites/depart/inspect>

- U.S. Secret Service, <www.treas.gov.usss>

nor anyone else in your household made. Ask to have the account(s) cancelled and a new one(s) opened.

- Get in touch with the IRS if someone has filed a fraudulent tax return using your personal and financial information. Call 877-777-4778 or go to <www.treas.gov/irs/ci>.
- If you think that someone has filed for bankruptcy using your name, contact the U.S. Trustee for the region where the bankruptcy was filed. For contact information go to <www.usdoj.gov/ust>.
- If you believe that the theft of your identity involves your securities, contact the appropriate brokerage or investment firm, file a complaint with the Securities and Exchange Commission at <www.sec.gov/complaint.shtml>, or call 202-942-7040.

Good Recordkeeping Is Essential

As you can see, dealing with identity theft can be quite time consuming and may require that you get in touch with many different businesses and government offices. On top of that, each of them will have their own process for dealing with your problem. Therefore, good recordkeeping is essential to helping you keep track of whom to contact—including the person's name, title, and contact information—what you must do, what the business or government office says it will do for you, and all relevant dates and deadlines.

Whenever you speak with someone by telephone and that person agrees to do or not do something related to the theft of your identity, follow up with a letter restating the agreement. Make a copy, mail it via certified mail, and request a return receipt. Keep the receipt with the rest of your records.

Retain copies of any letters you send or receive related to the theft of your identity. If you attach documents (correspondence, account statements, and the like) to the letters you send, be sure they are copies, not originals.

11

Now That
You Have It

Lois Nelson had been a client of mine more than a decade ago. Back then, she was a recent college graduate with an entry-level job in a large public relations firm. Lois had made the mistake many new graduates do—she had applied for and obtained a lot of credit cards. They had been a huge temptation for her, and after just a few years of using credit cards to finance trips to the mall, vacations, and expensive meals out, Lois was unable to pay everything she owed each month. Ultimately, she filed for a Chapter 13 bankruptcy.

Today she sat in my office smiling, something I had not seen her do very often when she was in the midst of her financial crisis. Lois was smiling because she had managed to turn her life around. Not only had she completed her Chapter 13 bankruptcy and begun rebuilding her credit, but she had advanced in her career and now made a comfortable living. In addition, she had just gotten married.

Anticipating the life she and her spouse wanted to build together, Lois was anxious to learn all she could about how to avoid future credit problems. She knew that maintaining a sound credit record would be key to achieving the dreams she and her husband shared. Lois also recognized that despite her education and career success, she knew relatively little about how to make wise credit choices and how to manage her money responsibly.

I told Lois that I wished all my former clients would do what she was doing. I explained that many consumers who re-build their credit after financial difficulty end up in trouble again because of their lack of money management savvy. I then went on to talk with Lois about credit and provided her with a list of books and magazines to read. I also gave her the names and phone numbers of several nonprofit organizations that could offer her solid credit management information at little or no cost.

Avoiding credit problems after you've recovered from money troubles and rebuilt your credit requires that you understand how to evaluate credit offers and manage your use of credit wisely. This chapter will provide you with some of the basic informa-tion you need to maintain a solid credit history.

Strategies for Keeping Bad Habits at Bay

After you have rebuilt your credit and the memories of your money troubles have begun to fade, you may be tempted to re-sume some of the habits that contributed to those troubles and ruined your credit record. Those habits may include the following:

- Applying for and using multiple bank cards
- Allowing your credit card balances to grow and paying only the minimum due each month
- Running up the balance on your checking account credit line
- Overusing your ATM and debit cards
- Not saving enough

If you find yourself returning to your old, bad habits, stop and think about the danger. Recovering from serious credit prob-lems, even bankruptcy, is hard enough the first time but can be even more difficult the second time around, because most cred-itors will be much less willing to work with you if they think you didn't learn your lesson the first time.

If you don't already have a household budget or spending plan, develop one. If your plan is realistic and you stick to it, it will help you allocate your income so that you can meet your monthly obligations and live on what you make. If you have enough in your budget, allocate money to put in savings each month, even if only a small amount. Over time, as your financial situation improves, save more each month. If you can't afford to save any money or if you want to pay your debts off faster, take a second job or find a better-paying job. Having money in savings for the purchase of big ticket items or something special, like a nice vacation, will help you use credit less. Also, financial advisors recommend that you maintain enough money in savings to cover at least six months of your living expenses so that you will have funds to fall back on if you or your spouse loses your job.

If you need help developing a budget, the following resources may be able to help:

- *Your local CCCS office.* If you don't find a CCCS listing in your local phone book, call the National Foundation For Consumer Credit (NFCC) at 800-388-2227 for the number of an NFCC-affiliated debt counseling office near you. You can also go to the NFCC Web site at <www.nfcc.org>.
- *The nearest cooperative extension service office.* To find it, look in the local government listings of your phone book, or call the U.S. Department of Agriculture's Education and Extension Service office at 201-720-3029.
- *Your local community college or the adult education program* sponsored by your area's public school system or a local college or university.

If you are having trouble controlling your spending, you may have emotional problems with money. For help, consider scheduling an appointment with a mental health professional or attending the meetings of the Debtors Anonymous chapter near you. Using many of the same successful techniques developed by Alcoholics Anonymous, Debtors Anonymous helps you understand and overcome your inability to control your spending. If you don't find a phone number for Debtors Anonymous in your local phone book, go to <www.debtorsanonymous.com> or call Debtors Anonymous at 781-453-2743.

How Much Credit Is Enough Credit?

One or two national bank cards, perhaps one travel and entertainment card such as American Express, and a gasoline card are all of the credit cards you need. Keep the accounts with the best terms of credit and close all others by writing to each creditor's customer service or customer relations office. You can usually find that address on the back of your credit card statement. Do not send your letter and unwanted card to the address you use when you are paying your bills. Cut up each card you cancel.

After you have closed the accounts, wait a few months and then order a copy of your credit report from each of the national credit bureaus. Make certain that there is a notation for each account indicating that it was closed at your request.

The danger in having a lot of credit cards is that you may be tempted to use them. Also, current and potential creditors won't look kindly on you when they review your credit record and discover that you have a lot of credit cards, even if you haven't used some of them in many months or if some of those

---

WARNING

Avoid retail store charge cards because they tend to come with relatively high rates of interest. Also, nearly all retailers accept MasterCard and Visa so there really is no need to have a retail store charge.

cards have zero balances. As long as the accounts are open, creditors will be concerned that you will begin using them.

How Much Credit Is Too Much?

Avoiding a reoccurrence of your financial troubles also requires that you monitor how much credit you have relative to your monthly income. You should do this every six months. Even if you have just one credit card, you can develop money troubles if you overuse it relative to your income.

When you are applying for important credit, one of the criteria potential creditors will look at to decide whether to approve your application is the amount of credit you have relative to your income. If that ratio is too high, you may have difficulty obtaining credit at reasonable terms, even if you earn a very comfortable salary.

An easy way to assess whether you have too much debt relative to your income is to perform a simple financial self-audit using the industry standards creditors use to help them decide which consumers are good credit risks. If your ratios exceed these standards, you should reduce your debt. Reducing your debt may require that you trim your budget, take a second job, or do some freelance or consulting work on the side. Here are the ratios you should compare yourself to:

- *Debt to income ratio.* Your debt to income ratio for credit cards and loans (don't include your monthly mortgage or rent payment, utility payments, and any monthly tax payments you may make) is your total monthly debt payment divided by your total monthly income (including all regular, reliable sources of monthly income). If this ratio is under 20 percent, you're doing okay, but the lower the better. Ten percent or less is ideal. If your ratio is over 20 percent, watch out! Stop using your credit cards and concentrate on paying off your card balances. If it exceeds 35 percent, you are in the danger zone. Although some creditors will still work with you, you probably won't qualify for credit with consumer-friendly terms. If your debt to income ratio is in the danger zone, it's imperative that you begin an aggressive program to reduce your debt. Otherwise, an unexpected big expense, the loss of your job, or another major setback could be financially disastrous. Once you reduce your debt load, deposit the money you were paying on that debt in a savings or money market account each month.

* *Your monthly mortgage payment (including taxes and insurance) to your monthly gross income ratio.* When evaluating a mortgage loan application, mortgage lenders like to see a ratio in the 28 to 36 percent range. In other words, they don't want your monthly house payment to exceed 28 to 36 percent of your gross monthly income. If your ratio is higher than that and you want to purchase a home, you may have to come up with a larger-than-normal down payment and you may have to pay a higher-than-average interest rate. As a result, you may not be able to afford the type of home you want to buy, or you may not be able to finance one at all until you improve your financial situation.

Creditors Care about the Three Cs

When you apply for a bank loan, the bank will assess your creditworthiness using the three Cs: capacity, capital, and character.

* *Capacity.* Do you have the ability to repay the credit you want to borrow? To determine this, a creditor will look at the ratios described in the preceding section of this chapter, your employment history, your income, and your history of payments on any current and recent debts.
* *Capital.* What assets do you own that you can use to collateralize the credit you are applying for? Creditors are interested in your collateral even if you are applying for unsecured credit because they want to be sure that if you

don't meet your payment obligations to them, you have assets that they could use to get payment. Depending on how much you are borrowing, if you have no significant assets, creditors may be unwilling to give you credit or won't give you as much as you applied for. If they do give you credit, it will probably come at a higher-than-usual interest rate and possibly with other unfavorable terms as well.

- *Character.* Are you worthy of a creditor's trust? The creditor will make this assessment based on your payment history with other creditors. It may also look at your history of paying your rent, utilities, and phone bill.

Types of Credit Accounts

When you apply for credit, you will be applying for revolving, installment, or open 30-day credit. Understanding how each type of credit works will help you make certain that you use the right kind of credit when you want to finance a purchase.

Revolving or Open-End Credit

When a credit account is open end or revolving, you have a fixed amount of credit that the creditor will expect you not to exceed. Each month you will have to pay at least the minimum

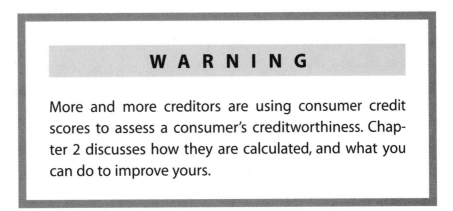

WARNING

More and more creditors are using consumer credit scores to assess a consumer's creditworthiness. Chapter 2 discusses how they are calculated, and what you can do to improve yours.

amount due on the account, which will be a percentage of the total amount that you owe. Examples of open-end credit include Visa and MasterCard cards, both secured and unsecured.

Installment or Closed-End Credit

If you are approved for this kind of credit, you'll borrow a fixed amount of money and the creditor will expect you to repay the debt in set amounts over a predetermined period. Examples of this kind of credit include the following:

- *Installment bank loans.* Your monthly loan payments will probably include principal plus interest with interest assessed from the date the loan is made. Your loan may or may not be collateralized, depending on how much you are borrowing and on your credit history.
- *Mortgage loans.* These are large installment loans with payback periods of up to 30 years. Your monthly payments on this kind of loan will include principal plus interest, and sometimes the cost of insurance and taxes for the property you are buying as well. The property collateralizes the loan.

Open 30-Day Credit

If you are approved for this kind of credit you can charge up to a certain limit, but you will be required to pay the full balance on your account each month or within 30 days of the billing date. Examples of this type of credit include:

- *Travel and entertainment cards,* such as American Express. With this kind of card you may get a higher credit limit than you get with a national bank card, as well as a variety of extra benefits. However, you may have to pay your balance in full each month, and if you don't, you will be charged a relatively high rate of interest. American Express also offers the Optima card, which lets you pay your card balance over time.

- *Oil and gas cards* are easy to qualify for. However, they often come with a relatively high rate of interest. Many oil and gas companies now offer revolving accounts.
- *Retail cards.* These cards may be open 30-day accounts or revolving accounts. They tend to have a higher rate of interest than national bank cards. State laws govern the terms of retail credit.

Evaluating Credit Offers

We are all used to receiving unsolicited offers for credit in the mail. We may also read ads for credit on the Internet. Some offers tout their low, low rates; others encourage balance transfers or offer frequent flier miles or points that can be used to purchase goods or services. Others promise that a portion of the annual fee or the account payments will go toward a charity.

To help you evaluate and compare various credit offers, return to Chapter 5, "Rebuilding Your Credit." Figure 5.1 in that chapter defines and explains some of the criteria you should consider.

Besides evaluating offers on the basis of their terms of credit, you should also consider how you intend to use the credit. Here are some questions to ask yourself in this regard:

- *Will I be paying the card balance in full each month?* If that is your intention, look for a card with no annual fee or a very low fee and with a long grace period—at least 25 days.
- *Do I intend to carry a balance on the card?* If you do, shop for a card with a low annual percentage rate, or APR. Also, be aware of how finance charges on a card will be calculated because some balance calculation methods are much more expensive than others. As a result, the method can significantly increase or decrease your overall cost of credit. Most companies use the *average daily balance with new purchases included* calculation method. This method is quite expensive for consumers.

The least expensive method for consumers is the *adjusted balance* method. Next best is *average daily balance, not including new purchases*. Other methods include *previous balance, two-cycle average daily balance excluding new purchases* and *two-cycle average daily balance including new purchases*, which is the most expensive balance calculation method. Read the fine print in a bank card offer to find out the card's balance calculation method.

* *What kind of credit limit do I need?* Don't opt for a card offer just because it comes with a high credit limit. Remember, using a credit card to finance a major purchase is an expensive way to buy something; applying for a bank loan or saving up so you can pay for the purchase with cash are wiser choices. Furthermore, if you have a high credit limit you may be tempted to charge up to that limit, which could not only get you into financial trouble again, but may make it difficult for you to obtain future credit you really need at reasonable terms—a mortgage loan for example.

* *Do I want other benefits with my credit card?* Some bank card companies market cards with such added benefits as product rebates, frequent flier miles, legal services, insurance, and so on. The problem with many of these cards is that you may have to charge a lot before you can actually take advantage of their extra benefits. Also, to get some of these benefits you may have to accept a high APR, an expensive balance calculation method, a short grace period, or some other unfavorable term of credit.

Some companies offer affinity cards, which typically bear the name or logo of a nonprofit organization or association. A percentage of each purchase made with an affinity card, or a portion of the annual fee, goes to the nonprofit organization or association. On the surface, using one of these cards may sound like a great way to support a cause you care about. However, most affinity cards cost more to use than other bank cards and the nonprofit organization or association you want to benefit by

> ## HOT TIP
>
> CardTrak produces a newsletter that contains information about the lowest rate credit cards, as well as information about the best deals on no-fee cards, affinity cards, secured cards, and so on. To obtain its current newsletter, send CardTrak a request letter together with a check or money order for $5.00. Mail it to CardTrak at PO Box 1700, Frederick, MD, 21702. You can also order the newsletter by calling CardTrak at 301-631-9100 or by visiting its Web site <www.cardtrak.com>.

using the card may not actually receive very much from the deal, although some cards are better than others. If you really care about a particular cause, you're probably better off writing it a check.

Credit Card Traps

Credit card solicitations may sound attractive until you read the details. Many "good" offers are actually bad deals for consumers and big money makers for a credit card company. For example, here are some of the things to check out when you read the fine print in a credit card offer. You want to avoid cards with these terms.

- A high annual fee or an annual fee that escalates after a period of time.
- A provision that allows for increases in a card's APR if you exceed your credit limit or don't make a payment on time. The increases can be substantial.

- A high penalty for being late with a payment. Take note of how late you can be before the penalty will be assessed. Some creditors will allow you to be a full month late before you will be charged a late fee, but others will charge a fee if you are just one day late.
- A fee for exceeding your credit limit. The fee may be a one-time fee or you could be charged a fee every month until you are no longer over your limit.
- A transaction fee. This is a fee that some credit card issuers charge each time you use a card.
- A fee if your check to the credit card company bounces.
- Cash advance fees.
- Offers that tout an especially low interest rate—a "teaser" rate—to encourage you to transfer your outstanding balance on one card to the lower interest card.
- An introductory low rate that lasts for a very short time and then moves to a much higher rate.
- High balance transfer fees. Ideally you should be able to transfer balances for no cost.

Take the Offensive

To get the best deal on a card, don't wait until you receive a bank card solicitation in the mail. Actively shop for the best

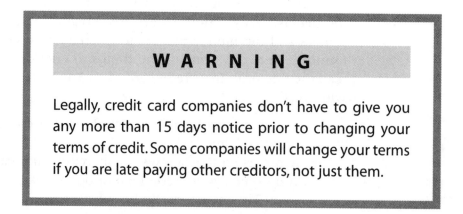

WARNING

Legally, credit card companies don't have to give you any more than 15 days notice prior to changing your terms of credit. Some companies will change your terms if you are late paying other creditors, not just them.

> ## HOT TIP
>
> If the terms of the bank card you already have are not as attractive as some of the offers you've received in the mail or find out about from Web sites, ask your current bank card company to meet or better the terms of the other cards. If you have a good payment record with the company, it may be willing to work with you rather than lose you as a customer.

deal and then apply for the card that you want. The Internet has made shopping for a bank card easy. For example, two independent sites you can visit to do that are <www.bankrate.com> and <www.cardtrak.com>.

Cash Advances Are Expensive

It may be tempting to get a cash advance from your credit card, especially if you are having trouble paying your bills or are hit with an unexpected expense that you don't have the money to cover and you cannot use a credit care to pay for the expense. Think long and hard before you do, however, because cash advances are expensive. For example, you may have to pay a higher interest rate for a cash advance than you pay for purchases that you charge, and the credit card company will probably start charging interest on the advance as soon as you receive it. In addition, you may have to pay a cash advance fee. Obviously, if you can't make ends meet, getting a cash advance is a quick and easy solution to your problems but, given its cost, you risk making your financial situation worse.

Do You Need Credit Life Insurance?

Credit life insurance ensures that if you die and there is an outstanding balance on your card, the insurance will pay it off. Although the amount you must pay each month to buy this kind of insurance may not seem like very much, credit life insurance is usually a colossal waste of money and tends to be one of the most expensive kinds of insurance you can buy. You are much better off taking the money you would use to purchase credit life insurance and using it to build up your savings faster.

A credit card company may send you information that seems to indicate that, to qualify for a particular credit card, you must purchase credit life insurance. Usually, the insurance is not really mandatory. The credit card company is just hoping that you will think it is, because the company can make more money by selling it to you.

Debit Cards

Debit cards have become a popular way to pay for goods and services. Although they often look exactly like a MasterCard or Visa, debit cards function more like a check—but with a few important differences.

HOT TIP

If you are worried about how your debts will get paid when you die, speak with your life insurance broker and with your estate planning attorney. You should also discuss how your bills would be paid if you were temporarily disabled because of an accident or illness.

> ### HOT TIP
>
> If you secure a loan with real estate or with some other asset that could be damaged or destroyed, your creditor may require that you purchase property insurance. However, you don't have to purchase it with the insurance company that the lender may be affiliated with. You should shop around to get the best price.

Debit cards can be used in two ways: online and offline. When you use an online debit card, you enter a security code or PIN (personal identification number) into a computer terminal at a retail or grocery store, and the cost of your purchase is debited immediately from your checking, savings, or brokerage account. Therefore, there is no delay or "float" as there is when you write a check.

If you use your debit card in an offline transaction, you run your card through the computer terminal, press credit rather than debit, and sign a receipt just as though you were using a credit card. It will take between one and three days for your

> ### HOT TIP
>
> Some banks have begun sending customers replacement ATM cards that are actually debit cards.

account to be debited for the purchase, just as if you paid with a check.

Obviously, using a debit card to pay for your purchases is more convenient than writing checks. However, debit cards have some drawbacks.

- If you don't keep an accurate record of your debit card purchases, you may quickly overdraw your account or spend more than you realize.
- Because credit cards and debit cards look so much alike, you may forget that you are using a debit card and that you don't get a month or so to pay for your purchase.
- There may be fees associated with using a debit card. In fact, your bank as well as the merchant may charge a fee for each use. The fees could significantly increase the cost of your purchase. Read your debit card agreement to find out about your bank's fees. Also, your bank may allow you to make a set number of debit card transactions at no charge but will charge if you exceed that number.
- There is no way to stop payment on a purchase.
- The Fair Credit Billing Act (FCBA) does not protect you if you pay for something with a debit card and there is a problem with the merchandise or service you purchased. The FCBA applies to credit card purchases only. Therefore, rather than withholding payment for the purchase while your dispute is being resolved, you will have to work out your problem directly with the business.
- Compared to a lost or stolen credit card, the Electronic Funds Transfers Act provides you with less protection if your debit card is lost or stolen. If your debit card is lost or stolen, and assuming you report its disappearance to your bank within two business days, you will be liable for a maximum of $50 in unauthorized charges. If you take longer, you could be legally obligated to pay as much as $500. However, if you don't realize that your debit card is missing until your bank statement arrives, you will have 60 days after the statement date to report that someone

has used your debit card without your permission. If you do, you can only be held liable for $50 in unauthorized charges and withdrawals. Otherwise, you are out of luck and will liable for all unauthorized charges. Furthermore, whoever has been using your debit card without your permission could completely drain your bank account.

Federal Laws You Should Know About

Chapter 8 discussed the Equal Credit Opportunity Act, a federal law that is important to women. You have also learned about the Fair Credit Reporting Act in this book. However, there are two other federal laws you should know about when you apply for or use credit, no matter what your gender. They are the Truth in Lending Act and the Fair Credit Billing Act.

The Truth in Lending Act (TILA)

The TILA helps you make an informed decision when you are comparing your credit options. The law requires creditors to provide in writing certain information to help you understand the full costs of the credit you are considering. You must be provided this information before you sign a credit agreement. Among other things, the creditor is obligated to tell you the following:

- The credit's monthly periodic interest rate
- The annual percentage rate, or APR, associated with the credit
- Any grace period that may be applicable
- The balance calculation method for purchases
- Annual fees, transaction fees for cash advances, late fees, and any other fees that apply to the card

The TILA also limits your liability if you lose a credit card or if it is stolen. The rules that apply to lost or stolen credit cards were discussed in the section of this chapter on debit cards.

If a creditor violates your rights under the TILA, you can sue for actual damages and twice the finance charges in the case of certain credit disclosures. If you win your lawsuit, the court may award you no more than $1,000 and no less than $100. You will also be able to collect court costs and attorney fees. Class action suits are permitted by the TILA. Meet with a consumer law attorney who has experience handling TILA lawsuits to find out if you have a strong case against a creditor. Don't try to handle the lawsuit on your own.

The Fair Credit Billing Act (FCBA)

The FCBA can help you resolve any billing problems you may have with a bank card, retail charge card, or with a line of credit. (It does not apply to billing problems with closed-end, or installment, accounts.) Examples of problems that would be covered by the FCBA include the following:

- You discover charges on your credit card billing statement that you don't understand, or you aren't being properly credited for payments you made.
- Your billing statement shows the wrong dollar amount for a credit purchase you made, or the statement for your line of credit is inaccurate. For example, it may show that you accessed more credit than you believe you did, or it may not reflect a payment you made.
- Your billing statement reflects charges you don't think you or an authorized user made.
- Your credit line statement shows that you accessed that credit line, but you don't believe that you or anyone authorized to do so used it.
- You are charged for goods/services you didn't accept or that you returned.
- You are charged for goods that are different from those you ordered.
- Computational errors were made in your billing statement.

Write—Don't Call

If you discover a problem in your billing statement, write—*do not call*—the appropriate creditor about the problem within 60 days of the date that the statement was mailed. If you call about the problem, the FCBA will not protect you. In your letter, be sure to include your name, account number, and a description of the problem as well as the date and amount of the error and an explanation of why you believe that the credit billing statement is incorrect. Indicate in your letter that you are exercising your legal rights under the FCBA, and be sure to date the letter. Make a copy of your letter for your files, and attach a copy of the billing statement about which you are complaining to the original letter. Then mail it certified with a return receipt requested. Send your letter to the billing errors or billing inquiries address listed on your statement; do not include it in the same envelope as your payment.

The creditor must acknowledge your letter within 30 days of receiving it, unless the problem has already been resolved by that time. Also, within 90 days, the creditor must either provide you with a written explanation of why the statement you received is correct and provide you with proof that it is correct, if you ask for it, or the creditor must correct the problem.

In the Meantime

While you're waiting to hear back from the creditor, you don't have to pay the amount in question or any finance charges related to it. Nor can the creditor report your account as delinquent, threaten to damage your credit record, sue you for payment, or close or restrict your account. However, the creditor may apply the amount you are disputing against your total credit limit. Also, you must continue paying on any other charges unrelated to the one you are disputing.

If Your Creditor Claims That Your Billing Statement Is Correct

The FCBA requires the creditor to notify you in writing if it concludes that your statement is correct. The law also says that you must pay what you owe the creditor, including applicable finance charges, within ten days of the notification. If you don't, the creditor can begin reporting to credit bureaus that your account is delinquent. If you continue to contend that your account billing statement is in error and you continue to try to get it corrected, the creditor must report that your account is in dispute when it reports to credit bureaus.

If the Creditor Says That Your Billing Statement Is in Error

If the creditor finds that you are correct about the error in your credit billing statement, it must credit your account, and you won't have to pay any late fees or finance charges related to the amount you were disputing.

Resolving Problems with Defective, Damaged, or Inferior Merchandise and Services

If you use a credit card to purchase a product or service and it turns out to be defective, damaged, or of poor quality, the FCBA allows you to take the same legal action against the company that issued you the credit card that you could take against the seller of the product or service under the laws of your state. For example, if your state says that you may withhold payment to the seller, or pay the seller and then sue for a refund, you might also be able to withhold payment to the card issuer. Before you do, however, you should consult with a consumer law attorney, especially since the FCBA says that you must make a serious effort to resolve your problem directly with the company that sold you the product or service before you take any legal action. The attorney can advise you about the best way to attempt to resolve the problem and build a written record of your efforts.

WARNING

The FCBA applies to defective, damaged, or inferior goods and services *only* if your purchase exceeds $50 and was made in your state or within 100 miles of your mailing address, unless the business that sold you the goods or services is also the card issuer. Therefore, the FCBA will probably not be much help if you do a lot of catalog or online shopping.

Federal Trade Commission Headquarters and Regional Offices

FTC Headquarters

6th and Pennsylvania Avenue NW
Washington, DC 20580
202-326-2222
202-326-2502 (TDD)

Northeast Region

Serves the residents of Connecticut, Maine, Massachusetts, New Hampshire, New Jersey, New York, Puerto Rico, Rhode Island, Vermont, and the U.S. Virgin Islands.

Northeast Region
Federal Trade Commission
1 Bowling Green
New York, NY 10004

Southeast Region

Serves the residents of Alabama, Florida, Georgia, Mississippi, North Carolina, South Carolina, and Tennessee.

Southeast Region
Federal Trade Commission
225 Peachtree Street NE, Suite 1500
Atlanta, GA 30303

East Central Region

Serves the residents of Delaware, District of Columbia, Maryland, Michigan, Ohio, Pennsylvania, Virginia, and West Virginia.

East Central Region
Federal Trade Commission
1111 Superior Avenue, Suite 200
Cleveland, OH 44114-2507

Southwest Region

Serves the residents of Arkansas, Louisiana, New Mexico, Oklahoma, and Texas.

Southwest Region
Federal Trade Commission
1999 Bryan Street, Suite 2150
Dallas, TX 75201-6808

Midwest Region

Serves the residents of Illinois, Indiana, Iowa, Kansas, Kentucky, Nebraska, North Dakota, Minnesota, Missouri, South Dakota, and Wisconsin.

Midwest Region
Federal Trade Commission
55 East Monroe Street, Suite 1860
Chicago, IL 60603-5701

Western Region

Serves the residents of Arizona, Northern California, Southern California, Colorado, Hawaii, Nevada, and Utah with two offices.

Western Region
Federal Trade Commission
901 Market Street, Suite 570
San Francisco, CA 94103

Western Region
Federal Trade Commission
10877 Wilshire Bouelvard, Suite 700
Los Angeles, CA 90024

Northwest Region

Serves the residents of Alaska, Idaho, Montana, Oregon, Washington, and Wyoming.

Northwest Region
Federal Trade Commission
2896 Federal Building
915 Second Avenue
Seattle, WA 98174

Index